18 INCHES

Scott,
may God richly bless you,
J Rey Addison
Susan C. Addison

Experiencing
the Mysteries *of* God
in the Journey *from*
Head *to* Heart

J. Ray Addison, PhD and
Susan C. Addison, PhD

18 Inches: Experiencing the Mysteries of God in the Journey from Head to Heart

Italics used to show emphasis in Bible quotations are the author's.

ISBN-13: 9781937756857
ISBN-10: 1937756858

Library of Congress: 2013938332

Cover design by Connie Gabbert

We dedicate this book to our many clients who have allowed us the privilege to walk with them as they sought to be comforted, healed, and set free from the bondage of sin.

Their lives have been our classroom, where we have witnessed God replace lies with truth and make His children free indeed.

CONTENTS

PREFACE

FOR THOUSANDS OF YEARS a body of ancient sacred writings has drawn kings, wise men, mystics, scholars, and skeptics to its pages. In vain, they have sought to master its wisdom and control its power. During the long darkness of the Middle Ages, those few who could translate its words jealously guarded it, preventing all others from discovering its secrets. As myths and legends grew about relics that could impart immortality to the seeker, some discovered that it was not in a grail or ark that one could find eternal life, but in the pages of the book itself. For the book is the portal to the Giver of life.

The book is available to us today, but its words are often obscured by man-made traditions, limiting assumptions, and internal distractions. Even within its pages there is a parable describing those who attempt to read it—the parable of the sower:

> Behold, a sower went out to sow. And as he sowed, some seed fell by the wayside; and the birds came and devoured them. Some fell on stony places where they did not have much earth; and they immediately sprang up because they had no depth of earth. But when the sun was up they were scorched, and because they had no root they withered away. And some fell among thorns, and the thorns sprang up and choked them. But others fell on good ground and yielded a crop: some a hundredfold, some sixty, some thirty. (Matthew 13:3b–8)

The volume you now hold is intended for the seeker. It is intended for those who have never understood the book, for those who have understood but desire deeper roots, and for those distracted by anxiety and stress and overcome with despair and futility. It is intended to make the truths of the book more accessible and more experiential. The contents of these pages have been mined from the book and forged in the helplessness of the counseling office as individuals have sought answers to life's most complex problems and relief from anguish and pain. They have also been brought forth from the lives of the authors—out of the refiner's fire.

INTRODUCTION

"The secret of the Lord *is with them that fear him; and he will show them his covenant."*—Psalm 25:14, KJV

"And my speech and my preaching were not with persuasive words of human wisdom, but in demonstration of the Spirit and of power, that your faith should not be in the wisdom of men but in the power of God.

However, we speak wisdom among those who are mature, yet not the wisdom, of this age, nor of the rulers of this age, who are coming to nothing.

But we speak the wisdom of God in a mystery, the hidden wisdom which God ordained before the ages for our glory, but God has revealed them to us through His Spirit. For the Spirit searches all things, yes, the deep things of God."—1 Corinthians 2:4–7, 10

THERE HAVE ALWAYS BEEN those who seek knowledge as an end in itself. During the first two centuries after Christ, there arose a cult from within the church called the Gnostics. Their name comes from the Greek word for knowledge. These Gnostics searched for the deep knowledge of God, thinking that the knowledge of the mysteries of God would make them wise. God has shown us, however, that the mysteries of God cannot be discovered by man—they are instead revealed by God. To know His mysteries, we must first know Him. As we come to know Him as He truly is, we come to know ourselves as we truly are. The result, in contrast to the expectations of the Gnostics, is that the true knowledge of His mysteries makes us humble. In this state of humility, without pride and self-centeredness to blind us, we can recognize the wisdom He reveals to us.

> I do not want you to be ignorant of this mystery, brothers, lest you should be wise in your own conceits. (Romans 11:25)

What then is God's intention for giving us this book which is called the Bible?

> I have given them Your word . . . Sanctify them by Your truth. Your word is truth. (John 17: 14, 17)

God's intention is to reveal truth. Why would God frame truth in a mystery?

> In that hour Jesus rejoiced in the Spirit and said, "I thank You, Father, Lord of heaven and earth, that You have hidden these things from the wise and prudent and revealed them to babes. Even so, Father, for so it seemed good in your sight." (Luke 10:21)

God's intent is to reveal truth in a world blinded by pride and deception. To reveal truth in such a way that those who desire truth for the purpose of power will be unable to decipher it. To reveal truth in such a way that only the childlike and humble will be able to recognize it; only the teachable will be able to learn it.

> Blessed are the meek, for they shall inherit the earth. Blessed are those who hunger and thirst for righteousness, for they shall be filled. (Matthew 5:5–6)

The mysteries of God are truths for which we have no frame of reference in our human experience; concepts that are foreign to human thought and that reach beyond human limitations. Paul, describing the apostles (the eyewitnesses of the life, death, and resurrection of Jesus Christ) said, "Let a man so consider us, as servants of Christ and stewards of the mysteries of God" (1 Corinthians 4:1). So then, we see that pride or desire for control interferes with recognizing truth from God. It follows that those who find truth are most likely to discover it in the depths of helplessness.

> And Jesus said, "For judgment I have come into this world, that those who do not see may see, and that those who see may be made blind." (John 9:39)

The human mind is uncomfortable with mysteries—it feels a compulsion to solve them. We attempt to pigeonhole knowledge revealed from Scripture into man-made systems of belief. The danger we encounter in this search is pride, as we trust our human intellect rather than submit to the Holy Spirit as our teacher. We tend to get God's intended sequence backwards, seeking to master the content of the Scriptures so that we can understand God. Instead, God intends for us to first know Him so that He may open our minds to understand the Scriptures and accurately apply them to our lives.

> And they said to one another, "Did not our heart burn within us while He talked with us on the road, and while He opened the Scriptures to us?" (Luke 24:32)

> But the Helper, the Holy Spirit, whom the Father will send in My name, He will teach you all things, and bring to your remembrance all things that I said to you. (John 14:26)

In this book, we seek to trace the hand of God as He lovingly directs and manages the events of our lives to take the truths of the Bible beyond mere theological or religious concepts. He seeks to make these truths experiential reality that brings us face-to-face with the living Christ. He opens our eyes not to a system of belief, but to see His face. This same God who, through Jesus, bridged the vast chasm between heaven and earth also knows what each of us needs to take these truths the eighteen inches from our head to our heart. As He works this mystery in our lives, we discover that we are coming to know Him more intimately and trust Him more deeply.

> *"But grow in grace, and in the knowledge of our Lord and Saviour Jesus Christ."*—**2 Peter 3:18a (KJV)**

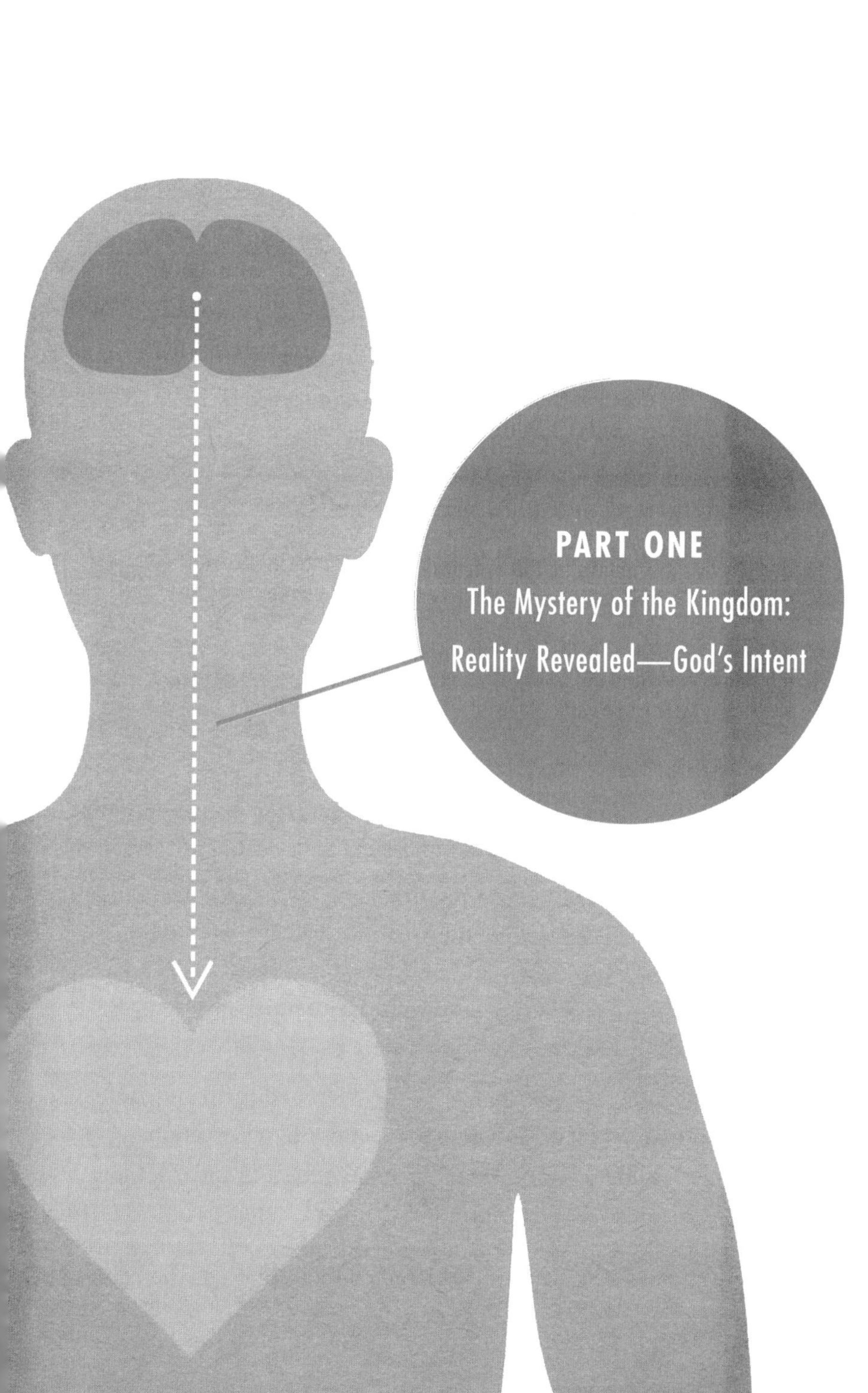

PART ONE

The Mystery of the Kingdom: Reality Revealed—God's Intent

> *"And the disciples came and said to Him, 'Why do You speak to them in parables?'*
>
> *He answered and said to them, 'Because it has been given to you to know the mysteries of the kingdom of heaven, but to them it has not been given. And in them the prophecy of Isaiah is fulfilled, which says:*
>
> *'Hearing you will hear and not understand,*
> *And seeing you will see and not perceive;*
> *For the hearts of this people have grown dull.*
> *Their ears are hard of hearing,*
> *And their eyes they have closed,*
> *Lest they should see with their eyes and hear with their ears,*
> *Lest they should understand with their hearts and turn,*
> *So that I should heal them.'"*—Matthew 13:10–11, 14–15

THE FIRST FORM THE GOOD NEWS TOOK was a proclamation that the kingdom of God was at hand.

> In those days John the Baptist came preaching in the wilderness of Judea, and saying, "Repent, for the kingdom of heaven is at hand!" (Matthew 3:1–2)
>
> Now after John was put in prison, Jesus came to Galilee, preaching the gospel of the kingdom of God, and saying, "The time is fulfilled, and the kingdom of God is at hand. Repent, and believe in the gospel." (Mark 1:14–15)
>
> Now when he was asked by the Pharisees when the kingdom of God would come, He answered them and said, "The kingdom of God does not come with observation; nor will they say, 'See here!', or 'See there!' For indeed, the kingdom of God is within you." (Luke 17:20–21)

In the Lord's Prayer, Jesus instructed us to pray for the coming of the kingdom:

> Your kingdom come.
> Your will be done
> On earth as it is in heaven . . .
> For Yours is the kingdom and the power and the glory
> forever. (Matthew 6:10, 13b)

Just as the first proclamation of the gospel references the kingdom, so too does the last verse of the book of Acts, recording the culmination of the ministry of the apostle Paul:

> Then Paul dwelt two whole years in his own rented house, and received all who came to him, preaching the kingdom of God and teaching the things which concern the Lord Jesus Christ with all confidence, no one forbidding him. (Acts 28:24)

Kingdom is a word rich in meaning. In this biblical context, *kingdom* does not refer to a place, but instead to a state: the state of being under the authority of the king. Where the king is, the kingdom follows. The kingdom is about the reign of the king, the protection of the king, the person of the king, relationship with the king, the love of the king, the will of the king—the rule of the king. This rule will eventually manifest as a literal kingdom when "the kingdoms of this world have become the kingdoms of our Lord and of His Christ, and He shall reign forever and ever!" (Revelation 11:15b).

The kingdom of God encompasses the reign of the sovereign King over the universe He created. The phrase "the kingdom of heaven" is found only in the gospel of Matthew and has special significance to the nation of Israel as it refers to the prophesied messianic kingdom. The kingdom of heaven describes God's rule on earth—it is heaven's rule on earth.[1] In the gospel of grace, we are invited to personally participate in the kingdom of God even before the kingdom of heaven is manifested on the earth.

We can understand the distinction in terms of scope and sequence—space and time:

- The kingdom of God is eternal; the kingdom of heaven unfolds in time.
- The kingdom of God is over all creation; the kingdom of heaven is on the earth.
- The kingdom of God describes the fact of the universal authority of God; the kingdom of heaven describes the restoration of the experience of God's authority among mankind, starting with Israel and culminating with all nations of the earth (Revelation 11:15; 19:11–20:6).

We experience the kingdom of God when the will of the indwelling God becomes the will of the individual; we will experience the kingdom of heaven at a point in time when the will of God will also be applied corporately to all matters of government and conduct.

The gospel of the kingdom is addressed to all (Romans 10:12). For the Jews it had special significance in that they were anticipating Messiah as king, as one who was coming to overthrow their Gentile oppressors and rule on the throne of David in Jerusalem in fulfillment of the prophecies of Scripture. Jesus corrected this expectation by explaining that before the restoration of the literal kingdom of the Messiah on earth, there had to be a restoration of the rule of God in each individual heart (Romans 6:12–14; 1 Peter 3:15). Before the liberation of Israel from bondage, each heart must be liberated from bondage. As He told the Jewish Pharisee Nicodemus:

> Jesus answered and said to him, "Most assuredly I say to you, unless one is born again, he cannot see the kingdom of God . . . Most assuredly I say to you, unless one is born of the water and the Spirit, he cannot enter the kingdom of God. That which is born of the flesh is flesh and that which is born of the Spirit is spirit." (John 3:3, 5–6)

One aspect of this mystery is that each individual, Jew and Gentile alike, is offered an invitation into relationship with the King before He returns to establish His literal kingdom on earth. For those who accept this invitation, not only do they enter the kingdom, but they will reign with the King when he returns (Romans 8:16–17; 2 Timothy 2:12; Revelation 20:6).

> For the kingdom of God is not in word but in power.
> (1 Corinthians 4:20)

The kingdom, then, is about control. The coming of the kingdom refers to the restoration of dominion or control to the King, with all the benefits that He brings. When we are under the authority and control of the King, the King assumes responsibility for us.

Jesus demonstrates this responsibility in His prayer of intercession for His disciples:

> While I was with them in the world, I kept them in Your name. Those whom You gave Me I have kept. (John 17:12a)

Since the kingdom is about God's control, our experience of God's kingdom is about trust. In this context, trust is the opposite of control. The model for trust that Jesus offered is the trust of a child.

> "Assuredly, I say to you, whoever does not receive the kingdom of God as a little child will by no means enter it." (Luke 18:17)

How can we experience this kind of trust?

John Bowlby was a leading researcher of early childhood personality development. Bowlby discovered that the first developmental task or milestone in the life of a child is attachment to his or her caregiver. The secure attachment of the child to the caregiver is the foundation upon which future relationships rest. How do we recognize secure attachment?

Bowlby explains that secure attachment is marked by the child's expectancy of response from the caregiver. He found that this kind of childhood trust depends on the following conditions:

- Is the caregiver accessible?
- Is the caregiver willing to respond, especially as comforter and protector?
- Am I acceptable in the eyes of my caregiver?[2]

Entering the kingdom of God like a child suggests that we have been convinced by God that:

- He is accessible. "I am with you always, even to the end of the age"(Matthew 28:20b). "He will not leave you nor forsake you" (Deuteronomy 31:6; Hebrews 13:5).
- He is willing to respond as comforter and protector. "Call to Me, and I will answer you" (Jeremiah 33:3a). "Ask, and it shall be given to you; seek, and you will find; knock, and it will be opened to you" (Matthew 7:7). "And I will pray the Father, and He shall give you another Comforter, that he may abide with you forever" (John 14:16, KJV). "I will fear no evil; for You are with me; Your rod and Your staff, they comfort me" (Psalm 23:4b).
- You and I have been made acceptable in His sight, and we are precious to Him. "Just as He chose us in Him before the foundation of the world, that we should be holy and without blame before Him in love" (Ephesians 1:4). "He who did not spare His own Son, but delivered Him up for us all, how shall He not with Him also freely give us all things?" (Romans 8:32). "My sheep hear My voice, and I know them, and they follow Me. And I give them eternal life, and they shall never perish; neither shall anyone snatch them out of My hand" (John 10:27–28).

What a marvelous description of true faith displayed in the trust of a child!

The problem is that our human nature desires to control—we are not comfortable turning control over to our King. But unlike God, we do not have complete knowledge of the truth about ourselves or the world we live in. We do not know how to accurately interpret the events of our past, the circumstances of our present, or the choices that affect our future. We are limited by our own perceptions of reality and the confines of our own experience in a very small part of time and space. We are also limited by our assumptions about reality, such as the assumption that if we cannot see, hear, or feel something, it does not exist.

The Forms of Control

This desire to control can be recognized in two forms. To the degree that we can maintain the illusion of control, we tend to become arrogant, self-centered, demanding, rigid, and manipulative. When we are faced with helplessness or loss of the control we desire, we may feel pain, guilt, worry, anger, or despair. In relationships, this desire to control most often takes the form of manipulation. Manipulation can take many forms, including intimidation, guilt, threats, bribery, flattery, or pressure to conform. Although we may not recognize it in subtle forms, these attempts to manipulate ultimately culminate in oppression. We are familiar with overt oppression, ranging from schoolyard bullying to the tyranny of the ruthless dictator. All too often, however, we fail to recognize covert oppression—the pressure applied within marriages, families, churches, workplaces, and neighborhoods.

Oppression can take place at all levels. Anywhere there is opportunity for power, there are those who will seek to grasp it. How can one distinguish between spiritual leadership in the home and manipulation, between love and coercion? How can we recognize control in the church—in committees, in ministers, in elders and deacons? How can we see past the rationalization of good intentions to recognize selfish human motives? When do the restrictions and covenants in a neighborhood association stop being protective and become instruments of oppression motivated by a desire to impose conformity—when instead of being guidelines for responsibility, they are used as instruments of control? When does supervision in the workplace become an opportunity for power over others? How do we recognize when government officials (town, county, state, or nation) have crossed the line from being public servants to seeking power as an end in itself?

Power is a dangerous drug. No one is immune to its potential for addiction—from the lowest board or committee member to the highest positions in government. How can we protect ourselves from this insidious threat? How can we endure the vulnerability that comes from relinquishing power and replacing it with trust? The answer lies not in philosophy, psychology, sociology, political science, or even religion. The answer is more complicated than these disciplines can fathom and yet more simple than they can accept. The answer lies hidden in the mysteries of the kingdom: the mystery of how God transforms our will into His will, of how our desire for control is replaced by trust in Him.

THE MYSTERY OF HIS WILL

> *"Blessed be the God and Father of our Lord Jesus Christ, who has blessed us with every spiritual blessing in the heavenly places in Christ . . . having made known to us the mystery of His will, according to His good pleasure which He purposed in Himself."*—Ephesians 1:3, 9

TO BEGIN THIS JOURNEY, we need to sort the concerns of life into two piles (like laundry day). One pile contains the things over which we have some control, and the other pile contains the things over which we have no control. Imagine drawing a circle around yourself that represents the limits of your control—all that you actually have any control over. When you find the outer limits of your control, you will discover that this circle is a fixed boundary. That is, since we are finite rather than infinite, there is a limit to our control. We usually find this boundary by painfully running up against it.

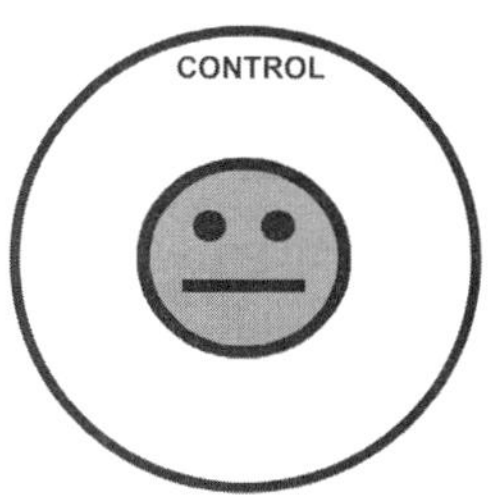

Once we have marked this boundary, our goal is to align a second boundary or circle with it. This is the circle of responsibility. The circle of responsibility, unlike the circle of control, is not fixed. It is flexible—it can expand beyond the circle of control or shrink inside it.

Our goal is to keep the circles in alignment. This means that we assume responsibility only for that over which we actually have control.

Circles of Control and Responsibility

> We, however, will not boast beyond measure, but within the limits of the sphere which God appointed us—a sphere which especially includes you. (2 Corinthians 10:13)

We can itemize the content of our circles in four categories: what we do, what we say, what we think, and what we feel. (For the scriptural basis of these categories, see actions in Genesis 4:6–8, James 1:22–25, 2:12–13, 3:13, and 4:17; 1 Peter 1:13–19, and Galatians 6:7–8; words in James 3:1–12 and Matthew 12:35–36); thoughts in Proverbs 23:7, Romans 12:1–3, Philippians 4:6–8, and Colossians 3:2), and feelings in Genesis 4:6–7, Psalm 146:5–9,

Proverbs 23:17–18, and 1 John 3:18–21.) This is all we have any control over in life. You may think of this diagram as a visual version of the Serenity Prayer:

> God grant me the serenity to accept the things I cannot change; the courage to change the things I can; and the wisdom to know the difference.

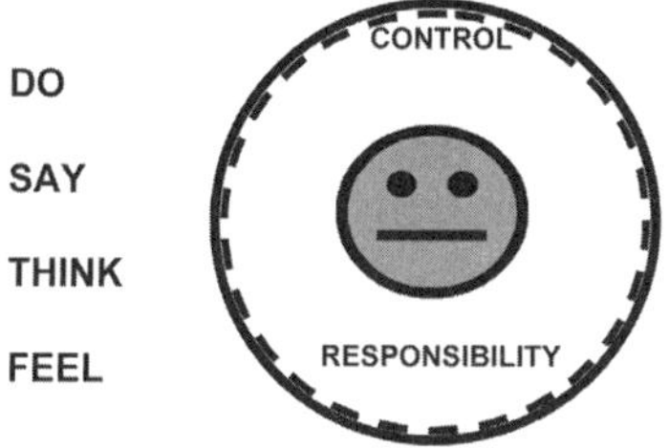

To the first three categories, we have direct access. We can access what we do (behavior, actions, and decisions), what we say, and what we think (beliefs, self-talk, mental images, perceptions, and our interpretation of experiences). To what we feel, however, we have only indirect access. Our feelings are influenced by choosing what we think, what we say, and what we do. Feelings are more dependent on our perception of events than they are on the events themselves.

Perception is a term used to describe how we as individuals view the world. Imagine a pair of French doors between you and the world. Through those doors comes all of the information you have about the world. The information comes to you in a form skewed by deletions, distortions, and generalizations. For example, as a child you are introduced to a four-footed furry creature with a tail, which is called *dog*. In the beginning, you have no concept that there are over two hundred breeds of dogs registered with the American Kennel Club. You therefore are missing information, in the form of deletions, as to the specific breed, characteristics, and purpose of the dog you know. Information is also missing in the form of generalizations. Are *all* four-footed furry creatures with a tail called dog? As you encounter this four-footed furry creature with a tail, you are also subject to interpretations, or distortions, about its use. In some parts of the world, dogs are seen as a food source. In other parts of the world they are seen as service animals and are used as herding dogs, tracking dogs, or rescue dogs. Dogs are also seen as pets and companions. In summary, a dog comes through your French doors with deletions, distortions, and generalizations.

As you encounter this dog, you form your own deletions, distortions, and generalizations about dogs. For example, if the dog is threatened by you, it may growl and snarl at you. If that frightens you, you may respond to all dogs with fear and believe they are going to growl and snarl at you or even hurt you. In doing so, you have created a generalization about dogs: that all dogs growl and snarl threateningly. This is coupled with deletions about how and when and under what circumstances dogs do growl and snarl, distorted by your fear upon encountering a threatened dog which growled and snarled at you. Your view of dogs, formed in all of these ways, is your perception.

As an old story goes, a young bride serves her first big Sunday dinner. She labors intensely to cook a pot roast in two separate pots while also managing the vegetables and salad for the dinner. Her husband becomes curious and questions why she cut the pot roast in half and used two pots to cook it. She does not know why she did it that way, other than that was the way her mother taught her to cook pot roast. They decide to ask her mother about this curious choice. Her mother replies, "That is what my mother taught me." Finding no real explanation for such a procedure, they go to Grandmother to ask her why she cut the pot roast in half and cooked both halves separately. Astonished by the question, Grandmother replies that she did that because she only had two pots, neither of which was large enough for the whole roast.

This story serves to illustrate how deletions, distortions, and generalizations can affect our perceptions about what is fact, what is necessity, or what is invention in the world around us. Consciously or unconsciously, we all interpret the experiences of our lives in light of what we believe and the context in which events happen. Our perceptions of our own motives and behaviors as well as those of others determine our ability to recognize the boundaries of control and responsibility in relationships.

Our interpretations, based on our perceptions, make aligning our circles very challenging. Our perceptions can cause us to read bad intentions into the behavior of others or to take some comment as a personal attack or criticism when it was not intended to be. On the other hand, distorted perceptions can cause us to ignore or rationalize intended attempts to manipulate us. Perceptions usually involve assumptions. A wise mentor used to frequently remind us that when dealing with people, we should assume nothing.

The task of keeping our circles in alignment would be easier if we lived in isolation like hermits; but as we have seen, it becomes very challenging when we are in relationship with anyone who matters to us. Now imagine a second set of circles of control and responsibility that represent your significant other—your spouse, child, parent, boss, coworker, or someone else with whom you are in relationship.

The problem occurs when an item from our significant other's circle of control is left on our doorstep—just outside our circle of control. This is something he or she does, says, thinks, or feels, something that matters to us and may affect our lives, but over which we have no control. The first response of our human nature is to try to exert some control over this thing. We try to expand our control circle to take this in, but our circle will not budge—it is like a brick wall.

At this point, our unconscious mind plays a trick on us. Since the circle of *control* will not move—we cannot possibly control this thing—we expand the circle of responsibility to take in this concern instead. Now we have created the illusion of control. It doesn't actually change anything, but temporarily we can deceive ourselves into thinking that if we try hard enough and long enough, we can make this thing change.

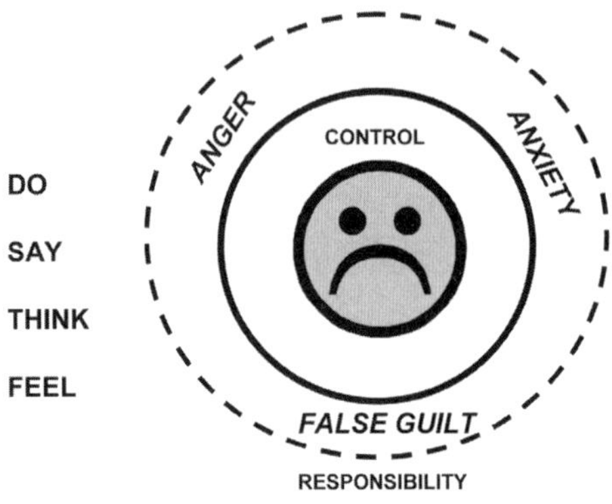

Illusion of Control

Now the circle of responsibility has expanded beyond the circle of control, opening up a gap between our control and that for which we feel responsible. This is the stress gap. This gap acts like a vacuum, sucking in stress over that for which we feel responsible. Stress is composed of three powerful emotions: anger, anxiety, and guilt.

Anger usually comes in the form of frustration. The thoughts that accompany frustration often take the form of demands or expectations that cannot be met. For example, "You've got to do something," "Make it stop," or "Make it happen."

Anxiety accompanies imagining the worst-case scenario. "What will happen if you can't fix this?" *Guilt* in this model is false guilt, because we are feeling guilty for something over which we have no control. Thoughts that accompany false guilt usually take the form of accusations, such as "You shouldn't have let this happen" or "You have failed as a ________________ [wife, husband, or parent]." Susan calls this the COWS syndrome. *Could've, Ought've, Would've,* and *Should've* are the four words of accusation, false guilt, or regret.

As stress accumulates, we can feel the pressure it creates. Now, in addition to whatever was bothering us to begin with, we are feeling the pressure from stress. The only way our unconscious mind knows how to deal with stress is to try harder, so the circle of responsibility is expanded farther. This expansion creates room for more frustration, anxiety, and guilt. The resulting scenario is like an overinflating balloon, with the inevitable consequence: it reaches a breaking point.

Something unexpected happens when this balloon pops. Rather than the circles returning to alignment, where what we can control and what we take responsibility for are one and the same, we experience a pendulum effect in which the responsibility circle collapses inside the control circle to the same degree that we had overextended responsibility.

The resulting condition is the opening of a gap in the opposite direction. The circle of responsibility is now inside the circle of control—meaning there are things in our lives we could be controlling but are not. We are now convinced that a situation or person is controlling what we do, say, think, or feel. Perception can create deception. This perception creates the opposite deception of the illusion of control, which is the illusion of helplessness. We develop the mindset of a victim, convinced that there is nothing we can do to change what we are feeling or doing. Ours is a state of powerlessness.

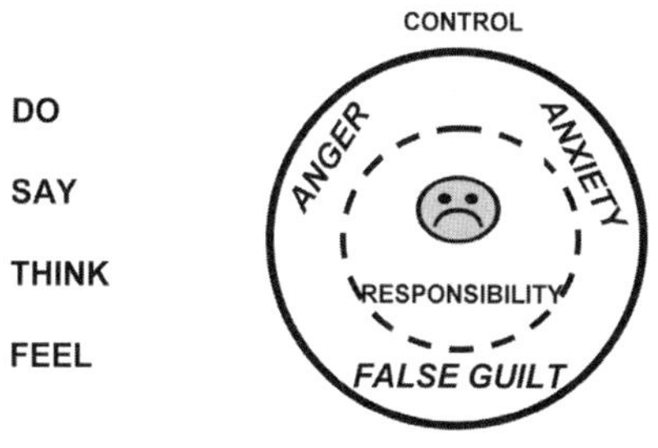

Illusion of Helplessness

Interestingly, the same stress will fill this gap, along with the same feelings: anger, anxiety, and guilt. In this case the difference is the object of the feelings. The anger and anxiety are perceived as being caused by someone or something outside our circle. "He is making me angry," "This situation is making me anxious," "I can never be happy until this changes." We convince ourselves that we are doomed to be unhappy as long as this situation or person remains unchanged. The guilt takes the form of shame, which results from powerlessness. Shame is feeling guilty for *being* rather than feeling guilty for *doing*. Shame is feeling inadequate, unacceptable, or defective, with the implication that there is nothing we can do about it.

In this gap, we feel like a victim. We feel trapped. We may even sink into depression. If it continues long enough, we may become desperate and seek an escape from the trap. If we perceive the trap to be a job, the escape looks like quitting. If the trap takes the form of a marriage, the escape looks like divorce or an affair. If the trap is perceived as life in general, the escape looks like suicide. In any event, the escape is not seen as a mere option to be considered, but as the only way to stop the misery. Even in the escape, the perception is that of "I have no choice."

This mindset of helplessness is a precursor to regret. Often this condition can feel like a polarity between two extremes of "I have to" and "I want to"—between obligation and joy. In this state we tend to experience deprivation, which in turn leads to overindulgence. We may perceive that our lives are ruled by responsibilities, such as a demanding job or caring for children. The point of desperation may take the form of indulging some pleasure, engaging in activities such as binge eating, drinking to excess, buying sprees, pornography, or affairs. The resulting feelings may take several forms. We may feel anger in the form of resentment: "I deserve this pleasure—this is the only thing in my life I have control over, and I won't give it up!" The behaviors may involve secrecy, with resultant anxiety about being discovered. We may feel chronic guilt and shame over behavior we ourselves find unacceptable, yet over which we believe we have no control.

Our human nature tends to cycle back and forth to varying degrees between the two extremes of overresponsibility and helplessness. Personality differences also contribute to our spending more time on one side of the pendulum than the other. Some of us, by personality, tend to be overly responsible. We spend most of our lives "inflating" until we reach a breaking point and crash into helplessness. Others of us are by nature more avoidant or passive. We eventually overreact to victimization with desperation. This overreaction then creates consequences that overwhelm us and cause us to retreat back into passivity.

How can we stop the pendulum, close the gaps, and live in alignment? Since the feelings generated by the stress gaps are the same in both scenarios, we can make them work for us. As anger, anxiety, and guilt grow more noticeable, they can serve as warning indicators, like the warning lights on the dashboard of a car. When these light up, it is our signal to stop and look under the hood. As we recognize increasing anger, anxiety, or guilt in our lives, we can then ask two questions:

1) For what am I feeling responsible?
2) To whom does it belong?

When we have identified that for which we feel responsible, we can check it against our list of responsibilities (what we do, say, think, or feel). If it belongs to us, we know we can access it, and we need only a plan for controlling it. If it belongs to someone else (what that person does, says, thinks, or feels), then we can transfer that responsibility to the one to whom it belongs. This exercise takes place in our mind; therefore, the other person does not have to accept responsibility in order for us to release it.

When we have successfully realigned our circles, we can feel the difference. When releasing responsibilities that are not their own and thus closing the stress gap, most people report feeling a sense of relief or the lifting of a burden. When reclaiming control over their own responsibilities, many people describe a feeling of empowerment or freedom.

The bottom line of this exercise is that control and responsibility go together. The more we try to control the things we cannot, the less control we have over the things we can.

What if we are feeling responsible for something from the past or the future which is not in our circle or the circle of any other person? In these situations, we become aware of one more circle—God's circle.

At this point, some would prefer the concept of "god" as they understand him, her, or it to be. The problem with this construct is that the resulting deity is limited by our understanding. Instead, we offer to the reader the historical concept of God as revealed and described in the Bible: one who transcends our understanding and possesses attributes that are absolutes to be accepted rather than propositions to be understood. Since the Bible describes one such attribute of God as omnipotence, His control circle includes everything, so we cannot draw it. We can only describe God's circle of responsibility in relationship to ourselves.

God holds us responsible for what we do, say, think, and feel (even though we will discover in further study that God gives us the grace or empowerment to carry out these responsibilities). God Himself retains responsibility for many other factors which affect our lives. Five of the items on God's list of responsibilities that we most often try to pull into our circles are the past, the future, justice, discovering our own sin, and being pleasing to Him.

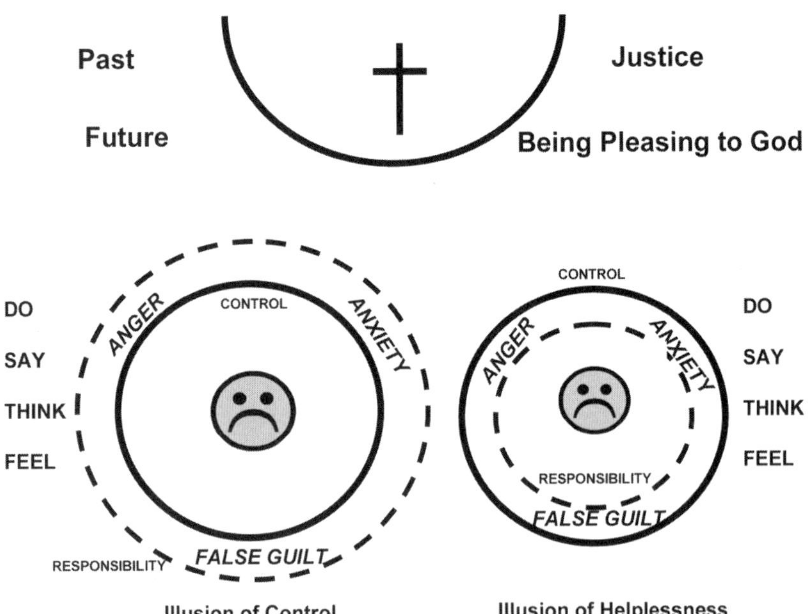

Illusion of Control

Illusion of Helplessness

The Past

We can recognize when we are attempting to control our past when we feel regret (guilt) or resentment (anger) and find ourselves saying, "If only ______________." "If only I knew then what I know now," for example. In effect, we are feeling responsible for changing the past. God invites us to transfer responsibility for our past to Him. He offers to redeem our past. In Romans 8:28, we read a beautiful promise:

> And we know that God causes all things to work together for good to those who love God, to those who are called according to His purpose. (Romans 8:28 NASB)

In the book of Genesis, Joseph has been sold into slavery by his brothers out of envy. He is sold to one of Pharaoh's court officials. After fending off the advances of his master's wife, Joseph is falsely accused by her and thrown into Pharaoh's dungeon. There, he endures until he is brought out to interpret Pharaoh's dream. Having done so, he is promoted to regent of Egypt, second only to Pharaoh, and put in charge of all the food supplies in Egypt to prepare for the famine of which Pharaoh dreamed. During this famine, Joseph's brothers come to Egypt to buy food. Joseph recognizes them, but they do not recognize him. After testing them and discovering they have changed, he reveals his identity to them.

Later, after the death of their father, they fear that Joseph will seek revenge for what they had done to him. Instead, Joseph says,

> Do not be afraid, for am I in the place of God? But as for you, you meant evil against me; but God meant it for good, in order to bring it about as it is this day, to save many people alive. (Genesis 50:19–20)

God can take what was intended for evil and use it for good. He can redeem our past. What we read in the story of Joseph and in Romans

8:28 is an invitation from God to put our past in His circle. He goes beyond just healing past wounds and comforting past traumas. He wants to take the things that seemingly should never have happened and use them for our good and His glory. (*Glory* refers to revealing God as He truly is.)

During the exodus of Israel from Egypt, a king hired a sorcerer named Balaam to curse the Israelites who were passing through his land. No matter how hard the sorcerer tried, every time he tried to pronounce a curse, God intervened and forced him to bless the Israelites instead.

> Nevertheless the Lord your God would not listen to Balaam, but the Lord your God turned the curse into a blessing for you, because the Lord your God loves you. (Deuteronomy 23:5)

God can redeem our past because He dwells above time rather than just in time. C.S Lewis described this truth by comparing it to his writing a book.[3] The author is free to turn to the first chapter and rewrite something. From his characters' point of view, he has changed their past. In like manner, the author could change the ending, which would be his characters' future. From the author's perspective, it is all present. God *can* redeem our past because He is not limited by time. God *wants* to redeem our past because He loves us.

> But, beloved, do not forget this one thing, that with the Lord one day is as a thousand years, and a thousand years as one day. (2 Peter 3:8)

The Future

Often, we feel responsible for controlling our future. We may feel the need to guarantee a certain outcome or to prevent some feared calamity. Our human nature is tempted to believe that if we take all the right steps, we can manipulate the future. Even our relationship with God may degenerate into bargaining: "If I do this for You, then You will prevent bad things from happening to me and my family."

We can recognize that we are feeling responsible for controlling our future when we feel anxiety and hear ourselves frequently saying, "What if?" "What if this situation never changes?" "What if I lose my job?" "What if I get sick?" "What if I fail?"

In the gospel of Matthew, Jesus describes God feeding the birds of the air and clothing the lilies of the field and saying:

Therefore do not worry, saying "What shall we eat?" or "What shall we drink" or "What shall we wear?" For after all these things the Gentiles seek. For your heavenly Father knows that you need all these things.

> But seek first the kingdom of God and His righteousness and all these things will be added to you.
>
> Therefore do not worry about tomorrow, for tomorrow will worry about its own things. Sufficient for the day is its own trouble. (Matthew 6:31–34)

God is inviting us to give Him responsibility for our future provision while He gives us the grace to be responsible for what we do today. God invites us also to trust Him for future direction:

> Trust in the LORD with all your heart, and lean not on your own understanding; in all your ways acknowledge Him, and He shall direct your paths. (Proverbs 3:5–6)

For many of us, decision making can be a source of extreme anxiety. What a relief to trust God not only for the wisdom to choose wisely today, but also to direct the outcome of these choices tomorrow!

> For I know the plans that I have for you, declares the Lord, plans for welfare and not for calamity to give you a future and a hope. (Jeremiah 29:11, NASB)

What a marvelous and comforting promise! Yet, the context of this passage makes its impact even more meaningful. The people of Judah had been turning from the true God to idolatry and hedonism. They sought "gods" they could manipulate, in effect acting as their own gods. In so doing, they became so self-centered and engrossed in the illusion of control that they even sacrificed their own children for their comfort and prosperity:

> And they have built the high places of Tophet, which is in the Valley of the Son of Hinnom, to burn their sons and their daughters in the fire, which I did not command, nor did it come into My heart. (Jeremiah 7:31)

> . . . to cause their sons and their daughters to pass through the fire to Molech. (Jeremiah 32:35b)

Molech was one of the pantheon of false gods worshiped by the people of ancient Canaan. "Tophet" translates into "roaster" or "incinerator." The valley of Ben Hinnom is just outside Jerusalem. The sacrifice of the children seemed to be associated with the belief that this practice would avert natural disasters or secure deliverance from enemies.[4] Here is a demonstration of the illusion of control wherein people believed they could control or manipulate their gods and consequently control their own future.

In Jeremiah, however, we discover that this horrible practice is not described in reference to the ancient Canaanites, but has been adopted by the Jews of Jerusalem living in the time of the prophet. Although at first shocking, this description sounds eerily familiar when we realize that what is being described here is the choice made by individuals and couples to kill their innocent children with the intent of meeting their own needs and making their lives more comfortable and less stressful. Does not the current practice of abortion on demand reflect this same intent?

It is worth noting that this Valley of Ben Hinnom is the same place which in the New Testament is named with the Greek *Gehenna,* which in English is translated *hell.* The picture that emerges from this realization is that God has for millennia been working to prevent people from choosing hell. If we try to be our own god, we end up sacrificing the most important things in our lives to attempt to secure our own happiness. The path of self-centeredness leads to the Valley of Ben Hinnom—hell.

By the time Jeremiah wrote against this practice, God in His patience and love had for years sent prophets to confront these people with truth, remind them of His love for them, and urge them to return to Him. He warned them of judgment that would come. In their contempt and arrogance, they killed and abused these prophets and ignored their warnings. Jeremiah was the last messenger from God before this judgment. He spoke to them for twenty-three years. They mocked him and even threw him down a well.

The prophesied judgment came in the form of a terrible attack and siege of Jerusalem by the Babylonians in 597 BC. Most of the inhabitants were taken as prisoners to Babylon, where they lived in exile for seventy years. God dictates a letter to Jeremiah to be sent to the captives living in exile in Babylon—these people who were suffering the consequences of their own sin. It is to these people that God says, "For I know the plans that I have for you, declares the Lord, plans for welfare not for calamity to give you a future and a hope" (Jeremiah 29:11).

So we see that God's promises are not expressions of our merit but are expressions of His grace, even when it is not earned or deserved. God is saying that when this judgment has accomplished its purpose of bringing you back to Me, you can't imagine the blessings I have for you.

> Eye has not seen, nor ear heard,
> Nor have entered into the heart of man
> The things which God has prepared for those who love
> Him. (2 Corinthians 2:9)

Justice

Justice is another of God's responsibilities that we often try to take upon ourselves.

> Many seek the ruler's favor, but justice for man comes from the Lord. (Proverbs 29:26)

This does not mean that we should not seek justice in human courts, but that we need to recognize that God is the source of justice. It is like saying that we seek food in a grocery store, but we recognize that the store must get it from the farmer (and even the farmer depends upon God for rain and sunlight).

> Commit your way to the Lord, trust also in Him, and He shall bring it to pass. He shall bring forth your righteousness as the light, and your justice as the noonday. (Psalm 37:5–6)

When the offense is personal, the desire for justice can take the form of revenge. We feel a need to take revenge ourselves in order to be satisfied. God does not rebuke the desire for revenge, but instead tells us that revenge is His responsibility.

> Never take your own revenge, beloved, but leave room for the wrath of God, for it is written, "Vengeance is Mine, I will repay, says the Lord." (Romans 12:19, NASB)

This promise becomes the basis for personal forgiveness. Sometimes forgiveness is seen as finding a way to explain away or rationalize an offense, such as citing the perpetrator's troubled childhood or good intentions. This exercise may help us achieve understanding of the behavior and even pity, but it is not forgiveness as revealed in the Scriptures. Forgiveness does not mean condoning, accepting, rationalizing, or minimizing wrongs or injustices. Forgiveness is transferring the responsibility for justice (vengeance) to God. Like the collection of a debt, forgiveness removes the debt from our account and sends it to the collector's account. God instructs us to forgive one another as God in Christ has forgiven us (Ephesians 4:32). How did God in Christ forgive us? God forgave us by accepting the payment made by Christ on our behalf. Rather than minimize our sin, God showed us that our sin was so serious that the payment was death, the death of His only son. Forgiveness is simple to receive, but very complex to make possible.

Often the description of forgiveness in the Scriptures employs Hebrew or Greek legal terms (translated in such words as *judge, prosecutor,* and *advocate*).

> My little children, these things I write to you, so that you may not sin. And if anyone sins, we have an Advocate with the Father, Jesus Christ the righteous. And He Himself is the propitiation for our sins, and not for ours only but also for the whole world. (1 John 2:1–2)

In this sense, what God did to make forgiveness possible and available involved a legal process. "Propitiation" comes from a Greek word that refers to the Hebrew term for atonement. Literally, it refers to the mercy seat which formed the lid of the ark of the covenant. The word means "that which covers." The law of Moses prescribed that once a year; the high priest would enter the Holy of Holies (the inner chamber of the temple) and sprinkle the mercy seat with the sacrificial blood. This blood, which foreshadowed the blood of Christ, was to atone for the sin of the people of Israel. Christ is both our Advocate (defense attorney) and the sacrifice offered to atone (cover or pay for) our sin.

Correlating these terms, we can see a sequence of forgiveness revealed in 1 John 2:1–2. I am brought into a courtroom. God, the Judge, is on the bench. Satan, the prosecuting attorney (Job 1:6–11), accuses me to God (the judge) by citing the violation of the law, or in essence, the violation of God's righteousness. God confronts me with the charges ("What have you done?" Genesis 3:13). God the Holy Spirit reveals my sin to me. Upon fully understanding what He has shown me, I confess my sin (which means to agree with what God has revealed). God as judge proclaims me guilty; the sentence is passed; the penalty is decreed. Jesus Christ (my advocate or defense attorney) intercedes by declaring that He Himself has paid this penalty in full for my sin. God (the judge) asks me, "Do you accept this payment on your behalf?" I say, "Yes." The Judge pronounces that I am free to go.

Once an individual has initially accepted the gift of forgiveness and salvation offered by Christ, he or she is free from condemnation forever (Hebrews 10:14, Romans 8:1). When individual sins are pointed out as described above by the Holy Spirit, we remain free and forgiven whether we acknowledge them or not. However, by understanding and acknowledging the sins God reveals and the forgiveness He provides, we will no longer hold the sin against ourselves or others. Making God's forgiveness experiential frees us from continuing to experience guilt. If we don't experience His forgiveness, we are open to experiencing false guilt and continual accusation by Satan, the prosecutor.

> To the praise of the glory of His grace, by which He made us accepted in the Beloved. In Him we have redemption through His blood, the forgiveness of sins, according to the riches of His grace. (Ephesians 1:6–7)

When we accept His gift, God takes each of us to the cross and in essence says, "I accept Christ's payment for your sin. Your debt is paid and forgiven." So too, we can take one who has sinned against us to that same cross, where Christ is asking us, "Will you let Me pay you for what he or she did to you?" We are then free to say to the offender, "I accept His payment for your sin against me. You are forgiven; that is, your sin (debt) against me has been transferred to Christ." It only remains, then, for each one brought to the cross to respond to Him. Their sin can be dealt with only in one of two ways: they can stand before the Judge and pay for their own sin or they can accept Christ's payment on their behalf. Either way, God secures justice, and we are free to release the offense or debt over to Him.

Forgiveness, therefore, is not limited by our compassion or understanding. Rather, it derives from God's grace. Our forgiveness of others is made possible by His mercy and grace.

Discovering Our Sin: Diagnosis vs. Accusation

God assumes responsibility for revealing our sin to us. We cannot find our own sin, much less the sin of others. We can recognize the results of sin in our lives and the lives of others, but we cannot find the source. The source consists of beliefs—deceptions that are well hidden (Jeremiah 17:9; 1 John 2:15–16, 26; Romans 1:24–25; Romans 12:2; 2 Peter 2:13; Ephesians 4:21–25; John 8:44–45; Hebrews 3:13; Colossians 2:2–8).

Some have asked, "What about the conscience?" The conscience is indeed a valuable gift from God, provided for both believers and unbelievers. In order to expand his control and deceive people more effectively, Satan works to disable the conscience in the individual (1 Timothy 4:1–2). However, even when it is working, the conscience is limited in its abilities. The conscience functions like a metal detector. It alerts us to the presence of hidden sin. It cannot, however, show us specifically what the sin is—or for that matter, to whom it belongs. We have worked with many children who have experienced sexual abuse from trusted family members and feel guilty or ashamed for what they perceive as their own sin. The sensitive conscience of a child registers that he or she has experienced something evil, but the child does not realize that the evil is not from him or herself but from the perpetrator.

> And by this we know that we are of the truth, and shall assure our hearts before Him. For if our heart condemns us, God is greater than our heart, and knows all things. Beloved,

> if our heart does not condemn us, we have confidence toward God. (1 John 3:19–21)
>
> In contrast, when God reveals sin, He reveals the very "thoughts and intents of the heart" (Hebrews 4:12–13).

The most common word for sin in the New Testament Greek is *hamartia,* which literally means "missing the mark," as in archery. So let us think of sin in terms of self-deception: ways in which we have missed the truth about ourselves, about God, or about life.

> The heart is deceitful above all things,
> And desperately wicked;
> Who can know it?
> I, the Lord, search the heart,
> I test the mind,
> Even to give every man according to his ways,
> According to the fruit of his doings. (Jeremiah 17:9–10)

God alone is responsible for revealing our sin to us. Indeed, He is the only one who can find it and convince us of the truth about it, since that is the nature of deception—it is hidden. By the time we can recognize our sin, it has already produced obvious consequences in our life, and much damage has already been done. Self-deception limits our trust of God and our intimacy with God, as well as our ability to maintain relationships with others. (We will explore in more detail later how God uses both the prompting of the Holy Spirit—John 16:13—and the Scriptures—2 Timothy 3:16–17—to reveal or diagnose our sin.)

When God reveals the lies we have been believing, we feel true guilt: that is, a painful awareness of our error and yet relief at an accurate diagnosis of what is hindering our life. Notice the contrast with false guilt or shame, which are the result of accusation. Accusation is motivated by hatred; God's disclosure of our sin is motivated by love (Hebrews 12:4–11). The intent of accusation is to diminish our worth; the intent of God in revealing our sin is to free us from lies that blind or bind us. True guilt, like physical pain, is designed to be brief—to alert us to a specific threat or problem so that we may respond. When we respond, the guilt ceases. False guilt or accusation offers no opportunity for response and is therefore endless, without hope of remedy.

God's revealing of our self-deception results in an "aha!" moment: the discovery of truth, the solution of a mystery. Searching for our own sin is like trying to look through a keyhole into a room; we see only limited, disconnected fragments of the room's contents. We make assumptions about the fragments we see, draw conclusions about ourselves and our sin, then walk away discouraged. When God opens the door, the room is fully revealed to us; we can see the contents and how they interrelate. We see the full context of our beliefs and behaviors, our false assumptions are corrected, and we receive truth. The truth then sets us free (John 8:32).

When we try to find our own sin by human reason, we end up either oblivious of our sin and self-righteous or focused on some unacceptable behavior or attitude which is merely the symptom of sin. Without discovering the root, the sin continues and we are stuck with the recurrent guilt that follows. This exercise is merely self-criticism. When God reveals our sin, we receive instruction and enlightenment not just about ourselves, but about the mind of God. We are privileged to see a greater reality, which expands our understanding beyond the limits of our own mind to show us the mind of God (1 Corinthians 2:16). The result is not a preoccupation with our sin, but an awareness of greater truth.

> Who can understand his errors?
> Cleanse me from secret faults.
> Keep back your servant also from presumptuous sins;
> Let them not have dominion over me.

> Then I shall be blameless,
> And I shall be innocent of great transgression.
> Let the words of my mouth and the meditation of my heart
> Be acceptable in your sight,
> O Lord, my strength and my Redeemer. (Psalm 19:12–14)

> Have mercy upon me, O God,
> According to Your lovingkindness;
> According to the multitude of Your tender mercies,
> Blot out my transgressions.
> Wash me thoroughly from my iniquity,
> And cleanse me from my sin.
> For I acknowledge my transgressions,
> And my sin is always before me.
>
> Behold, You desire truth in the inward parts,
> And in the hidden part You will make me to know wisdom.
>
> Create in me a clean heart, O God,
> And renew a steadfast spirit within me.
> (Psalm 51:1–3, 6, 10)

Pleasing God

Who is responsible for making me and you acceptable and pleasing to God? Contrary to what we may think, God assumes that responsibility.

> For by grace you have been saved through faith, and that not of yourselves; it is the gift of God, not of works, lest anyone should boast. (Ephesians 2:8–9)

> As you therefore have received Christ Jesus the Lord, so walk in Him. (Colossians 2:6)

Many of us are familiar with the fact that our relationship with God begins by grace through faith, but we may be surprised by the revelation that it *continues* by grace through faith. Jesus said:

> Abide in Me, and I in you. As the branch cannot bear fruit of itself, unless it abides in the vine, neither can you unless you abide in Me. I am the vine, you are the branches. He who abides in Me, and I in him, bears much fruit; for without Me you can do nothing. (John 15:4–5)

To *abide* means to remain attached. We did not attach ourselves to Christ. He attached us to Himself.

> You did not choose Me, but I chose you and appointed you that you should go and bear fruit, and that your fruit should remain, that whatever you ask the Father in My name He may give you. (John 15:16)

"Abide" does not suggest perfect performance. "Abide" describes attachment—remaining in the relationship He initiated. The Greek word for "abide" means to stay in a given place, state, relation, or expectancy. Here we see a display of the truth that God's grace always precedes our response, and God's response grows our expectancy—which is faith.

Our responsibility is to abide; that is, to remain attached to Him. His responsibility is to bear fruit through us that is pleasing to Him. The fruit in one sense is described in Galatians 5:22–23:

> But the fruit of the Spirit is love, joy, peace, longsuffering, kindness, goodness, faithfulness, gentleness, self-control.

If we expect any of these traits to come from ourselves, we will in time be disappointed. If we desire any of these qualities, we can get them only from God. Notice that self-control is a fruit of the Spirit. This means that self-control is not control *by* self, but control *of* self *by* the Spirit.

> I have been crucified with Christ; it is no longer I who live, but Christ lives in me; and the life which I now live in the flesh I live by faith in the Son of God, who loved me and gave Himself for me. (Galatians 2:20)

> Being confident of this very thing, that He who has begun a good work in you will complete it until the day of Christ Jesus. (Philippians 1:6)

> For it is God who is at work in you, both to will and to work for His good pleasure. (Philippians 2:13, NASB)

> Now may the God of peace who brought up our Lord Jesus from the dead, that great Shepherd of the sheep, through the blood of the everlasting covenant, make you complete in every good work to do His will, working in you what is well pleasing in His sight, through Jesus Christ, to whom be glory forever and ever. Amen. (Hebrews 13:20–21)

It is humbling and reassuring to know that God doesn't even count on us to have the consistent desire, much less the ability, to please Him. He is working in us to generate the motive (will) to please Him and to accomplish through us the thoughts and behaviors that please Him. The result is that we have the assurance of being pleasing to Him, and He is glorified—revealed—in the process.

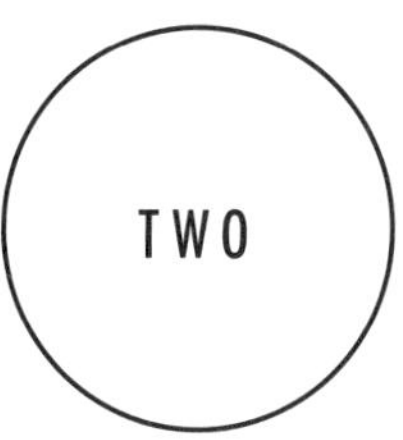

THE GREAT MYSTERY: THE CIRCLES IN MARRIAGE

> *"For this reason a man shall leave his father and mother and be joined to his wife, and the two shall become one flesh. This is a great mystery, but I speak concerning Christ and the church."*—Ephesians 5:31–32

THE RELATIONSHIP BETWEEN THE FIRST COUPLE, Adam and Eve, was intended by God to be based on trust. The description of them in Genesis 2:24–25, which was referenced by Paul in the Ephesians passage above, goes on to say, "And they were both naked, the man and his wife, and were not ashamed." This description portrays not only innocence, but also trust: transparency without deception or concealment, both toward God and each other. In the next chapter of Genesis, we read of the deception of this first couple by the serpent and the consequences that followed. By choosing not to trust God, they lost the intimate relationship they had with Him—the source of all life. This fact is illustrated by their attempt to hide from God (Genesis 3:8).

Once their relationship with God was broken, they could no longer trust each other. They made themselves coverings (Genesis 3:7). When the curse was fully realized, the woman was told by God, "Your desire shall be for your husband, and he shall rule over you"(Genesis 3:16b). This passage is often misinterpreted. The phrase "your desire shall be for your husband" does not reference love or affection. We can understand what this phrase really means by reading on in Genesis 4:7, where Cain is contemplating the murder of his brother, and God warns him, "And if you do not do well, sin lies at the door. And its desire is for you, but you should rule over it." The phrase describes a desire to control or possess.

It is evident here that for the first man and woman, trust was lost and replaced by the desire to control each other. So it remains to this very day in human nature: we trust only as far as we can control a person or a situation.

Trust, in any relationship, is linked to expectations. One use for the circles in marriage is to sort expectations. Am I expecting of my spouse things for which I am responsible, such as my feelings or my actions? Am I expecting of my spouse things for which God is responsible, such as security, protection, love, joy, identity, or purpose in life? It may be helpful to make a checklist of current expectations. We can most readily recognize these expectations when they go unmet, with the resulting frustration, anxiety, insecurity, or disappointment. Examples would include:

- "I expect you to make me feel loved."
- "I expect you to make me feel secure."
- "I expect you to make me feel respected."
- "I expect you to give me self-esteem."
- "I expect you to give me a sense of worth."
- "I expect you to give me identity [as a wife or husband]."

As we use the circle-defining questions "For what am I feeling responsible?" and "To whom does it belong?", we can sort these expectations accordingly. We alone choose how to respond to our spouse's behavior or words.

Examples of the illusion of helplessness and disempowerment resulting from our assigning away responsibility include:

- "He/she makes me so mad."
- "She/he drove me to drink."

- "My affair is my spouse's fault."
- "You killed my love for you."

We may not realize it, but we have a variety of responses from which to choose when we encounter unmet expectations, disappointments, or irritations. Keep in mind that when we transfer responsibility, we give away the control that goes with it. If we inappropriately shift blame by convincing ourselves that this person made us feel something or made us behave in a certain way, we are also giving that person control over our behavior or feelings. In light of this fact, the alternative to blame-shifting is empowerment. We are not responsible for what our spouse does or says to us, but we are responsible for how we respond to it.

A useful exercise for preventing a victim mindset is one we call "the price tags." It is based on a biblical model for decision making found in Luke 14:28:

> For which of you, intending to build a tower, does not sit down first and count the cost, whether he has enough to finish it?

This passage is set in the context of commitment to follow Jesus Christ in the face of adversity and hardship. When we find ourselves in a situation between the proverbial rock and hard place, where both options may involve painful or distressing consequences, it is a signal to stop and count the cost. A wise professor once told me that if you find yourself with only two options, you no longer have a choice—you have a dilemma. In a dilemma, our main concern is not long-term consequences, but immediate relief. Obviously this increases the risk of long-term regrets. It seems to be a feature of our human nature under stress to polarize our thinking into either/or scenarios. If we can discover at least one more option, the stress will be reduced, and we will be free to select a long-term solution. It is precisely in this context of distressing trials that God invites us to ask Him for wisdom in understanding and in finding alternatives:

> If any of you lacks wisdom, let Him ask of God, who gives to all liberally and without reproach, and it will be given to him. (James 1:5)

After listing all our options, we can then list the anticipated worst-case-scenario consequences associated with each option. This list becomes the "price tag" for each option.

Next, we list our top five values and priorities in life. That is, the non-negotiables in our lives—what we want in our epitaph, the things that reflect how we want to be remembered. We then use the priority list to comparison shop. The goal is to select the option with the least number of top priority items on the price tag. Once we select it, then we "buy" it.

Where this exercise proves most practical is when it comes time to pay the price for our choice—when the anticipated consequences arrive like a bill in the mail. We can now say, "This discomfort is part of the price I choose to pay to buy what is most important to me. This is me securing what matters most in my life." When we adopt this attitude, we find ourselves on top of the circumstances rather than under them, and regrets have been virtually eliminated.

The alternative problem scenario in marriage is to assume responsibility for our spouse's behavior. This usually manifests in the form of anxiety or false guilt.

- "If I meet your needs, I can make you love me."
- "If I avoid conflict, I can make you happy."
- "If I fail to satisfy you, you will leave me."
- "If you are unhappy, I must be failing [as a wife/husband]."

The solution here is to own responsibility for our behavior, words, and thoughts while transferring responsibility for our spouse's responses back to him or her.

The best way to discover misplaced responsibilities is effective communication, in which we express our expectations, sort our responsibilities, and negotiate our responses to each other. The end result is each spouse relating to each other with aligned circles, which allows for minimum defensiveness and maximum creativity. This phenomenon is sometimes called "maturity." Further, we are now in a position to recognize any of God's responsibilities we may be holding, and in releasing them to Him, we find the grace to respond with the fruit of His Spirit.

One of the most practical applications of these principles for believers is the realization that we are not asking ourselves to trust our spouse directly, but to trust God as the source for our expectations. This allows God the option of meeting our needs directly or channeling them through our spouse (much like the grocery store analogy mentioned earlier).

> Every good gift and every perfect gift is from above, and comes down from the Father of lights, with whom there is no variation or shadow of turning. (James 1:17)

God wants us to know that everything good we have ever received in our lives has come from Him. As we become convinced of Him as our source, our anxiety regarding our spouse's limitations diminishes and is displaced by peace.

The verse that opened this section spoke of a mystery regarding Christ and His relationship to the church in the context of the relationship of a man and woman in marriage. This describes a type of love that a husband is called upon to give that is of divine origin and is for that reason totally selfless. The response of the wife, as of the church, is one of trust. That is also of divine origin in that this kind of trust flows from grace. The marriage described here is foreign to the natural human condition. This kind of marriage can only exist in two individuals who are under the authority of Christ and have relinquished the attempt to control the responses of one other. If this proposition makes you anxious, then you are on the right track.

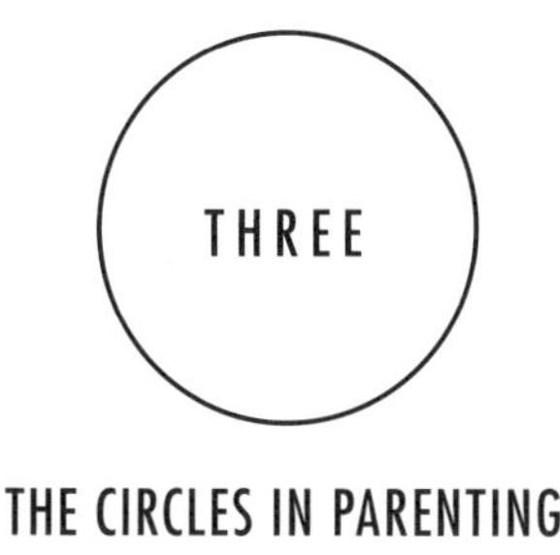

THREE

THE CIRCLES IN PARENTING

CONTROL AND RESPONSIBILITY GO TOGETHER. As one of my colleagues used to say, "If I accomplish nothing else in my parenting, I want my child to launch into adulthood with the understanding that responsibility brings freedom and irresponsibility brings restraints."

Victor Frankl was a Jewish psychiatrist in Austria when Hitler came to power. He was arrested and endured the horrors of several concentration camps, including Auschwitz. After his release he wrote an inspirational book: *Man's Search for Meaning.* In this book, he writes:

> Freedom is not the last word. Freedom is only part of the story and half of the truth. Freedom is but the negative aspect of the whole phenomenon whose positive aspect is responsibleness. In fact, freedom is in danger of degenerating into mere arbitrariness unless it is lived in terms of responsibleness. That is why I recommend that the Statue of Liberty on the East Coast be supplemented by a Statue of Responsibility on the West Coast.[5]

Imagine the implications for the future if an entire generation emerged with this conviction: to be free, we must be responsible. One practical method for implementing this principle in your parenting is by means of a simple contract. Lee Canter, in his book *Assertive Parenting,* provides an excellent format for this, with a contract of three columns: responsibilities, consequences, and freedoms.[6]

The first column is a specific and concise list of responsibilities expected of the child by the parents. These responsibilities are best described in concrete, behavioral, measurable terms. For example, "We expect you to put your dirty clothes in the hamper each day."

The consequences need to relate to the responsibility. Lee Canter describes natural consequences and logical consequences. The concept is that whenever it is safe and age-appropriate, the natural consequences of irresponsible behavior can provide the best education. For example, "Not putting your clothes in the hamper results in your not having any clean clothes when you need them." When natural consequences are not available, then we need to provide consequences that are logically related to the child's behavior. Specific time periods are designated for each expectation (the grading periods at school can serve for this purpose). For example, violating the set curfew during a semester causes an earlier curfew for the next semester. Although thinking of consequences will take time on your part, laying them out clearly will help to instill cause-and-effect reasoning in your child and prevents the problem of having to use grounding for every offense so that it becomes ineffective.

The freedoms can include things the child wants to be able to do. The contract thus provides a way for the child to earn as much freedom as he or she can handle by demonstrating responsibility over time in each area. This component helps keep the child motivated to use the contract. At the end of the designated time period, the consequences or freedoms are applied. For example, "Your responsibility in caring for your clothes during this grading period results in your getting new clothes. Your keeping your curfew during this semester has earned a later curfew for next semester."

Using this method, control and responsibility can be given to each child incrementally as he or she demonstrates readiness to receive it. This will result in delegating responsibility to match the increasing maturity of the child and hopefully help to minimize the common control struggles of adolescence. In other words, by the time the parents realize that they no longer have any real control over their child, the child will have had the opportunity to earn the parents' trust so that the parents' control is no longer necessary.

Another colleague of ours, Dr. Paul Warren, a behavioral pediatrician, has described how he and his wife relate each expectation of their children to a family value, such as trust, love, loyalty, integrity, respect, and commitment. For example, "It is important for you to be where you say you will be, because your doing so is about your integrity and our trusting you." This connection with values also models for the child what is worth getting upset about and what is not. (Of course, this requires the parents to apply this truth to themselves first.)

Another application of the circles to parenting involves establishing firm boundaries for ourselves. By accepting responsibility only for that which we can control (what *we* do, say, think, and feel), we can avoid the pitfall of seeing our children as extensions of ourselves. We can avoid seeing their behavior as a reflection on us and instead see it as being within their circle. The parent does not control the child's behavior, words, or thoughts. The parent controls the modeling, the teaching, and the consequences. To reframe our expectations of ourselves as parents, we can use a biblical model: the greenhouse.

> I planted, Apollos watered, but God was causing the growth. So then neither the one who plants nor the one who waters is anything, but God who causes the growth. (1 Corinthians 3:6–7, NASB)

Our task as parents is to create an environment that is protected from the elements and provides nutrients and exposure to the light. In other words, an environment that provides maximum exposure to the Holy Spirit. The result of understanding this is that we no longer see our children's behavior as a reflection on ourselves, so we are free to respond to it creatively and without defensiveness. At the same time, by transferring responsibility for our children's futures to God, we are freed from fear and overprotectiveness. We are free to respond to the present.

THE CIRCLES IN THE WORKPLACE

WHEN WE APPLY THE CIRCLES OF CONTROL and responsibility to the workplace, our focus will be on boundaries and expectations. We can start once more with an expectation checklist. What are we expecting of our job and our coworkers? Do any of these expectations belong in our circle? For example:

- "I expect this job to make me feel happy and fulfilled."
- "I expect this job to make me feel respected."
- "I have to work here; I don't have a choice."

How easy it is to slip into a victim mindset in the workplace! When we feel trapped, we tend either to sink into depression and despair or to become desperate. It is wise to remind ourselves that we choose what we do and what we feel. In these situations, we can employ the price tag exercise described earlier. List options, assign price tags, compare with our priorities and values, then "buy" an option.

Some expectations may belong in God's circle:

"I expect this job to give me significance—a sense of worth."
"I expect this job to give me security."
"I expect this job to give me identity."

In our culture, men especially have a tendency to define their identity by their jobs. Dr. Howard Hendricks once observed that when meeting one another, the second question a man usually asks after being told another man's name is, "What do you do?"[7] It is not wise to base our identity on anything that we can lose. This applies to jobs and marriages as well as to possessions.

> Do not lay up for yourselves treasures on earth, where moth and rust destroy and where thieves break in and steal; but lay up for yourselves treasures in heaven, where neither moth nor rust destroys and where thieves do not break in and steal. For where your treasure is, there your heart will be also. (Matthew 6:19–21)

A good exercise to reveal what we are depending on for our identity and security is to replace the word "treasure" in the above passage with "self-worth," "identity," or "security." The results can be useful in any context to reveal false sources of security, but we shall apply them here to the workplace.

Reclaiming ownership of expectations that are ours and transferring to God those that are His can greatly reduce tension in the workplace, increase our focus and productivity, and most importantly, enhance our job satisfaction.

God invites us to recognize that as His servants, we work for Him. In the context of a job, we are invited to reframe our experience as being on assignment from Him.

In our office, we have often used staffing agencies. This is an agency that employs various clerical personnel whom they send on temporary assignments to businesses like ours who need short-term office help. Although they work in our office fulfilling job descriptions we give them, they actually work for the agency and get their paychecks from it. These agencies are often called "temp agencies," and the personnel they send to us are referred to as "temporary employees." Perhaps the servant of God, while working in this life, is the ultimate temporary employee. A friend once said to me in describing his job, "It doesn't matter who signs my paycheck, I work for God. I answer to Him, and He is responsible for me."

Ephesians 6:6–7, although originally given in the context of slavery, can be applied to attitude in the modern workplace as well, where we can serve "not with eyeservice, as men-pleasers, but as bondservants of Christ, doing the will of God from the heart, with goodwill doing service, as to the Lord, and not to men." In the parallel passage in Colossians 3:23 we read, "And whatever you do, do it heartily, as to the Lord and not to men, knowing that from the Lord you will receive the reward of the inheritance; for you serve the Lord Christ."

> *"Here is what I have seen: It is good and fitting for one to eat and drink, and to enjoy the good of all his labor in which he toils under the sun all the days of his life which God gives him; for it is his heritage . . . For he will not dwell unduly on the days of his life, because God keeps him busy with the joy of his heart."*—**Ecclesiastes 5:18, 20**

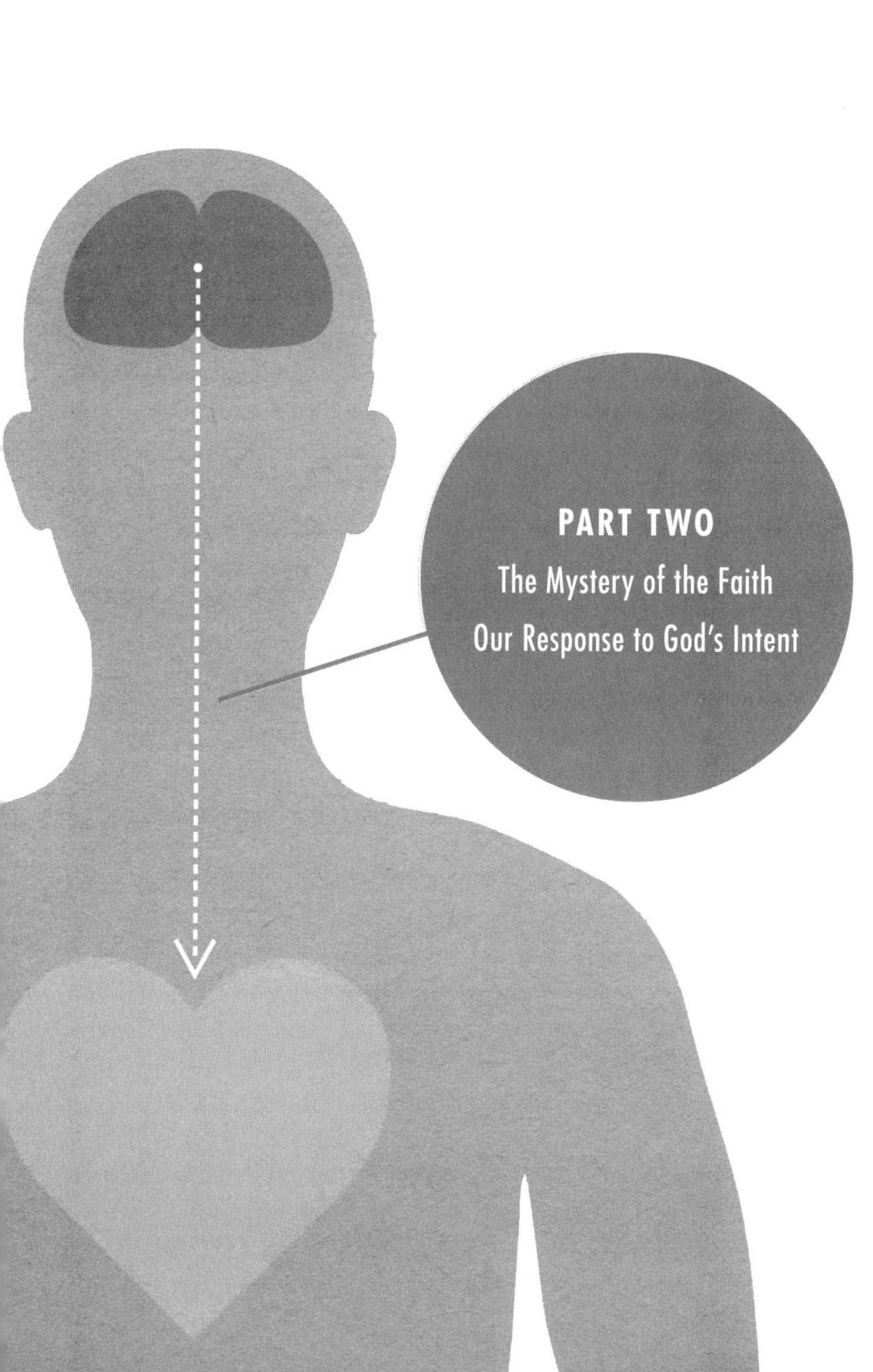
PART TWO
The Mystery of the Faith
Our Response to God's Intent

". . . holding the mystery of the faith with a pure conscience."
—1 Timothy 3:9

The circles of control and responsibility serve to reveal God's plan for our lives. After recognizing God's plan, our first response is usually, "How do I make this happen in my life? What steps do I take to appropriate God's plan? How do I make my faith stronger?"

This response reminds us of the original problem—that of attempting in our own abilities to do what only God can do. If God intends us to experience *His* control and *His* kingdom, then *we* cannot do anything to accomplish that goal. Our task is to receive something He gives us; to accept something *He* does in our lives. We are confronted with the concept of "faith."

Limited by our human nature, we assume faith is something we must do. We must somehow make ourselves believe something. The mystery of faith, however, has to do with God evoking a response from us. Perhaps the word *trust* would better capture the meaning of the Greek word *pisteuo,* which is usually translated as *faith* in English. For God trains our hearts to trust Him. The result is a response that is deeper than willpower or conscious thought. The result is a spontaneous response more akin to fear.

FIVE

THE FEAR OF GOD

MUCH CONFUSION SURROUNDS THE CONCEPT of the fear of God. Throughout the Scriptures, we are encouraged to learn the fear of the Lord.

> Teach me your way, O Lord;
> I will walk in Your truth;
> Unite my heart to fear Your name. (Psalm 86:11)

> Therefore, having these promises, beloved, let us cleanse ourselves from all filthiness of the flesh and spirit, perfecting holiness in the fear of God. (2 Corinthians 7:1)

Yet, in the first epistle of John, we are told:

There is no fear in love; but perfect love casts out fear, because fear involves punishment, and the one who fears is not perfected in love. (1 John 4:18 NASB)

Paul, writing to Timothy, observes:

For God has not given us a spirit of fear, but of power and of love and of a sound mind. (2 Timothy 1:7)

How can we reconcile these truths? Usually we are told that "fear" sometimes means fear and sometimes means reverence, but that explanation falls short of capturing the full impact of this concept.

Faith and Fear

There are three words in the Greek that are frequently translated by the English word *fear.* The word most used in the Scripture is *phobos,* from which we derive our English word *phobia. Phobos* describes fear or terror and is used in both good and bad contexts. The second word is *deilia,* which describes timidity, cowardice, or intimidation and is always used in a bad sense in the Scriptures. The third word is *eulabeia,* which relates to reverence or caution that is evoked by respect. It is always used in a good sense in Scripture.

In the passage from 2 Timothy, *deilia* is used. We then understand that God has not given us a spirit of cowardice or intimidation. This is the same word Jesus used in John 14:27 when He said, "Let not your hearts be troubled, neither let it be *afraid.*"

In the other passages cited above, the word *phobos,* or some form of it, is used. (In Psalm 86:11, *yawray,* the Hebrew equivalent of *phobos,* is used.) *Eulabeia,* or reverence, is used only seven times in the Bible. *Deilia,* or cowardice, is used about five times. *Phobos* is used over fifty times. The point is, if the intent of the author was to describe reverence, there was a Greek word for that purpose. Since there are a variety of Greek words to describe *kinds* of fear, the difference being revealed here is not in *kind* of fear but in the *object* of fear. The fear described in the Bible is a response determined by perception or belief. The 1 John 4:18 passage, for example, is describing not the fear of God but instead the fear of punishment.

We will fear whatever we are convinced controls our life. What we fear then becomes our god. Fear, therefore, is unconscious faith. The fear of God is being convinced of God's sovereignty. It is for this reason that David prays, "Unite my heart to fear Your name" (Psalm 86:11). Our hearts are divided or fragmented by fear of failure, fear of abandonment, fear of rejection, fear of pain, fear of poverty, fear of death, or fear of helplessness. How do we become convinced of God's control? How does He unite our hearts to fear Him alone?

As we saw in chapter 1, God takes responsibility to apply the truths of Scripture to the experiences of our lives, to train us to believe that His circle of control envelops our lives. To do this, however, He must first reveal what we mistakenly believe controls our lives. He allows situations in our lives which expose our fears. These fears reveal the false gods to which we have become enslaved. Inevitably, one of these gods turns out to be ourselves.

One of the metaphors which the Scriptures use to describe this process is the "furnace of affliction" or the smelting furnace.(Isaiah 48:10b, Psalm 66:10). This refers to an experience God allows in our lives in which we feel totally helpless. Further, we discover that our coping skills are not sufficient to deal with this helplessness, and we feel overwhelmed. In this state of helplessness, we have an opportunity to experience God's control in the midst of our weakness.

In 2 Corinthians 12:7–9, Paul described an affliction which he called a "thorn in the flesh." He prayed three times for God to remove this affliction. God's response was, "My grace is sufficient for you, for My strength is made perfect in weakness."

> My flesh and my heart may fail;
> But God is the strength of my heart and my portion forever.
> (Psalm 73:26, NASB)

How often we read this passage and fail to understand. We misinterpret it to mean that we are to pray for God to make us stronger in order to endure suffering in our own strength. Then we are shocked and disappointed when after we pray, we do not feel any stronger.

God's intention is not to make us strong, but to *be* our strength. In this way, we are nurtured and protected and He is glorified. Remember, to glorify is to reveal something for what it truly is. To glorify God is to reveal Him as He truly is.

There is yet more to the fear of the Lord. In the opening chapter of Job, we discover God proclaiming to Satan that Job "fears God." Satan responds:

> Does Job fear God for nothing? (Job 1:8–9)

The accusation is that Job fears God only as long as he is prospering. The implication is that Job's motive is selfish. Satan goes on to propose that if there were no incentive for Job to fear God, he would instead curse God. Job suffers severe grief and deep anguish in the loss of all that he has. By the end of this horrible experience, a marvelous thing has happened: God has come to Job and revealed Himself as He truly is. Job responds:

> I know that Thou canst do all things, and that no purpose of Thine can be thwarted . . . I have heard of Thee by the hearing of the ear; but now my eye sees Thee. (Job 42:1–2, 5, NASB)

Job is describing intimacy with God. Before this experience he knew about God, and even that God was sovereign. After this experience, Job says he knows God and that He is worthy of trust. Not only can no purpose of God's be thwarted, but His purposes can be trusted.

We see a sharp contrast here between the religiosity of Job's friends and the relationship of Job with God. His friends had come to him with the intention of helping him and the pretense of knowing how to help. Instead, they judged him and falsely accused him. They assumed they knew how to interpret Job's plight, Job's intentions, and God's will. Their admonitions were based on the belief that we can prevent bad things from happening to us by right living or good performance. This is the essence of the difference between those who truly fear God and those who fear punishment (1 John 4:18). That is, those who fear punishment trust in themselves to prevent it. Those who fear God trust His intentions and His control; they trust His love and grace. Job speaks to his friends:

> All my close friends abhor me,
> And those whom I love have turned against me.
> For I know that my Redeemer lives,
> If you should say, "How shall we persecute him?"—
> Since the root of the matter is found in me,
> Be afraid of the sword for yourselves;
> For wrath brings the punishment of the sword,
> That you may know there is a judgment.
> (Job 19:19, 25, 28–29)

It is all too common today for many in the church to react to similar situations with accusation and judgment. Often this reaction comes from fear. Like Job's friends, many of us are terrified by the prospect that something could come upon our lives which we are helpless to prevent or escape. We need to believe the lie that we can prevent or control any such threat. Therefore, we judge that the accused could have prevented this situation or at least could make the painful experience stop if he or she would only do the "right thing." The alternative, that we too could be overwhelmed by such pain or loss, is far too frightening for us to accept. The result is a religion of performance—the illusion of control. An even more frightening observation is that unwittingly, these "friends" of Job were used by Satan to carry out his agenda of accusing Job and tormenting him. Here is the principle that Satan will usurp any control that humans try to claim. There is no alternative: either we are under God's protective authority or we expose ourselves to Satan's control.

These experiences of helplessness are marked by spiritual doubt, frustration, or depression. Phil was a committed Christian who believed that if he faithfully followed biblical principles, he and his family would be blessed. Then came the day he lost his job. He tried desperately to find another job, but no one was hiring. He was convinced that he had failed to perform correctly for God and must still be missing whatever God was wanting him to do. He sank deeper and deeper into depression.

> But when I looked for good, evil came to me;
> And when I waited for light, then came darkness.
> My heart is in turmoil and cannot rest;
> Days of affliction confront me. (Job 30:26–27)

In the final chapter of Job, God Himself rebukes Job's friends:

My wrath is aroused against you and your two friends, for you have not spoken of Me what is right, as My servant Job has.

> Now therefore, take for yourselves seven bulls and seven rams, go to my servant Job, and offer up for yourselves a burnt offering; and My servant Job shall pray for you. For I will accept him, lest I deal with you according to your folly; because you have not spoken of Me what is right, as My servant Job has. (Job 42:7b–8)

Job, in this experience, grew into deeper intimacy with God. But even before the trial, he was described by God as one who "fears God and shuns evil." This observation is confirmed again by God in His statement that Job has spoken of God "what is right" in contrast to the confident declarations of Job's friends regarding God. Specifically, they knew facts about God but had not learned to trust Him. They did not realize that the facts about God they were attempting to use to convict Job did not apply to Job or his situation. Further, they were ignorant of the true nature and character of God.

To what was God referring when He spoke of Job speaking "what was right" about Him? Perhaps He was saying that "My servant Job knows that I love justice and that I do not forsake my loved ones (Psalm 37:28). My servant Job knows that I want him to expect justice from Me

(Proverbs 29:26). My servant Job knows that I want him to share with Me whatever is troubling his heart (Matthew 11:28–29). My servant Job knows that he can expect Me to answer whenever he cries out to Me (Jeremiah 33:3) and that I am near to all who call upon Me (Psalm 145:18). My servant Job knows that he can expect Me to comfort him (Psalm 71:20–21) and that I heal the brokenhearted and bind up their wounds (Psalm 147:3). My servant Job knows that he can expect Me to reveal truth to him (Psalm 143:7–8). My servant Job knows that I am not the author of confusion (1 Corinthians 14:33). My servant Job knows that I do not willingly afflict the sons of men (Lamentations 3:33). My servant Job responds to Me when I speak to him (1 Samuel 3:10)."

If someone were convinced that all these things were true of God, how would you expect that person to respond in such a situation of pain and helplessness?

> Let us therefore come boldly to the throne of grace, that we may obtain mercy and find grace to help in time of need. (Hebrews 4:16)

> The fear of man brings a snare,
> But whoever trusts in the Lord shall be safe. (Proverbs 29:25)

Notice the parallel established between "fear" and "trust" in the verse from Proverbs. When we know the fear of the Lord, we are convinced of God's sovereignty and equally convinced of God's love. He trains our hearts to trust Him. In this way, the fear of the Lord dispels the fear of all else. When He is finished, the only one we fear is the one we don't have to be afraid of—the One who loves us unconditionally and sacrificially. It is the difference between fearing the knife in the hand of an assailant and finding hope in the scalpel in the hand of the surgeon. This is the trust of a child who, although helpless, does not fear, because the child is not focused on his or her helplessness, but instead on the nearness of his or her parent.

> Be still, and know that I am God. (Psalm 46:10a)

The two Hebrew verbs in this passage are rich in meaning. The first, *raphah,* means to be still, let go, cease striving, even to be weak. In some contexts, it can mean to cause to heal. The second word, *yawdah,* means to know intimately and experientially. God is inviting us to cease striving to be our own gods and experientially know Him as God. We find the same message in the prophet Zechariah:

> So [the angel] answered and said to me:
> "This is the word of the Lord to Zerubbabel:
> 'Not by might nor by power, but by My Spirit,'
> Says the Lord of hosts."
> (Zechariah 4:6)

If you have heard the magnificent *Messiah* by Handel, you will be familiar with the ninth chapter of Isaiah. The prophet Isaiah foretold the coming of "Immanuel" in chapter 7 and describes Him as the "Prince of Peace" in chapter 9. This Prince will establish His kingdom and secure peace and justice for ever. In this context, we are instructed how to deal with present threats:

> You are not to say, "It is a conspiracy!"
> In regard to all that this people call a conspiracy,
> And you are not to fear what they fear or be in dread of it.
> It is the Lord of hosts whom you should regard as holy.
> And He shall be your fear,
> And He shall be your dread.
> Then He shall become a sanctuary.
> (Isaiah 8:12–14a, NASB)

Fear of the Lord, or spontaneous faith, is our response to God's grace. The biblical term *grace* comes from the Greek word for *gift* (*charis*) and describes God's gifts to us, which are motivated by His unconditional love. We come to trust in His work rather than our effort; His firm grasp on us rather than our ability to hold on to Him.

David demonstrates the fear of the Lord in his encounter with Goliath the giant. In the first book of Samuel, we find the armies of Israel "dreadfully afraid" of this intimidating warrior. It is no coincidence that this giant was a descendant of Anak. This is the same race of giants that struck fear in the hearts of the first generation of Israelites who had come out of Egypt in the exodus (Deuteronomy 1:28; 9:1–2). When twelve Israelite spies were sent into Canaan to investigate this land promised to them by God, they returned reporting that the land was indeed just as God had said: rich and bountiful. But ten of them reported that there were also giants in the land.

> There we saw the giants (the descendants of Anak came from the giants); and we were like grasshoppers in our own sight, and so we were in their sight. (Numbers 13:33)

As a result of this report, the people were overcome with fear. They refused to enter the land and receive the gift God had given them. Two of the twelve spies (Joshua and Caleb) challenged the report of the other ten by saying:

> Only do not rebel against the Lord, nor fear the people of the land, for they are our bread; their protection has departed from them, and the Lord is with us. Do not fear them. (Numbers 14:9)

The people did not listen but instead were ruled by their fear of man, and as a result they rejected the gift of God. They chose to believe what appeared to be true rather than what God said was true. Therefore instead of enjoying life in the promised land, they died in the wilderness.

Forty years later, when the second generation of Israelites (along with Joshua and Caleb) was given the same opportunity to accept the gift of the land, they believed God and took possession of it.

> And at that time Joshua came and cut off the Anakim from the mountains . . .
>
> None of the Anakim were left in the land of the children of Israel; they remained only in Gaza, in Gath, and in Ashdod. (Joshua 11:21a, 22)

So it was that Goliath of Gath, one of the Anakim, caused the armies of Israel to fear and tremble. David appeared to be no match for this warrior in size, strength, or skill. David, however, had been trained by God to trust God and not himself. When David offers to challenge this Philistine, King Saul expresses his doubt and observes that David is an untrained youth going up against a seasoned warrior.

> But David said to Saul, "Your servant used to keep his father's sheep, and when a lion or a bear came and took a lamb out of the flock, I went out after it and struck it . . .Your servant has killed both lion and bear; and this uncircumcised Philistine will be like one of them, seeing he has defied the armies of the living God."
>
> Moreover David said, "The Lord who delivered me from the paw of the lion and from the paw of the bear, He will deliver me from the hand of this Philistine." (1 Samuel 17:34–35a; 36–37)

When David confronts Goliath, he proclaims,

> You come to me with a sword, with a spear, and with a javelin. But I come to you in the name of the Lord of hosts, the God of the armies of Israel, whom you have defied. This day the Lord will deliver you into my hand . . . Then all this assembly shall know that the Lord does not save with sword and spear; for the battle is the Lord's and He will give you into our hands. (1 Samuel 17:45b–46a; 47)

God had trained David by allowing threats into his life. David in his helplessness learned by experience to trust God to deal with these threats. God in His faithfulness delivered David, proving to him that he need fear nothing but God. Fear is unconscious faith.

Faith and Authority

> For He taught them as one having authority, and not as the scribes. (Matthew 7:29)

Since faith involves what we perceive to be controlling our lives, there is a connection between faith and authority. This connection is shown in an encounter Jesus had with a Roman centurion. The centurion was attached to the army of occupation which the Roman Empire was using to govern the conquered territory of Israel and the surrounding region.

> So when he heard about Jesus, he sent elders of the Jews to Him, pleading with Him to come and heal his servant. And when they came to Jesus, they begged Him earnestly, saying that the one for whom He should do this was deserving, "For he loves our nation and has built us a synagogue."
>
> Then Jesus went with them. And when He was already not far from the house, the centurion sent friends to Him, saying to Him, "Lord, do not trouble yourself, for I am not

> worthy that You should enter under my roof. Therefore I did not think myself worthy to come to You. But say the word, and my servant will be healed. For I also am a man placed under authority, having soldiers under me. And I say to one, 'Go,' and he goes; and to another, 'Come,' and he comes; and to my servant, 'Do this,' and he does it."
>
> When Jesus heard these things, He marveled at him, and turned around and said the crowd that followed Him, "I say to you, I have not found such great faith, not even in Israel!"
>
> And those who were sent, returning to the house, found the servant well who had been sick. (Luke 7:3–10)

The centurion of Capernaum understood authority. He recognized in Jesus one who, like himself, was under authority. Notice that he said, "I also am a man placed *under* authority." Being under authority—that of the Roman Empire—made him an instrument of that authority. He knew that the control resided in the authority, not in the man. He was familiar with the limited authority of the empire which he served. So when he saw the works of Jesus and heard the words of Jesus, he knew that he was witnessing a far greater authority than that of Rome. He understood the difference between power and authority. In essence, he placed himself and his servant under that authority.

Shortly after this incident, Jesus and his disciples were crossing the Sea of Galilee when a storm arose. As the waves swamped the boat, the disciples, seasoned fishermen, knew they were in serious trouble. They no longer had any control over this threat. Jesus was actually sleeping during this storm.

> Then the disciples came to Him and awoke Him, saying, "Lord, save us! We are perishing!"
>
> But He said to them, "Why are you fearful, O you of little faith?" Then He arose and rebuked the winds and the sea, and there was a great calm.

> So the men marveled, saying, "Who can this be, that even the winds and the sea obey Him?" (Matthew 8:25–27)

In contrast to the response of the centurion, let us look at the response of the Roman provincial governor, Pontius Pilate, during the trial of Jesus. The centurion would have been a noncommissioned officer—a sergeant in today's military. Pilate was the supreme commander in the region of Palestine, appointed by the emperor, Tiberius. After questioning Jesus, Pilate discovered that the motive of those who had arrested Him was envy. He therefore wanted to release Him.

> The Jews answered him, "We have a law, and by that law He ought to die because He made Himself out to be the Son of God."
>
> When Pilate therefore heard this statement, he was the more afraid; and he entered into the Praetorium again, and said to Jesus, "Where are you from?" But Jesus gave him no answer.
>
> Pilate therefore said to Him, "You do not speak to me? Do you not know that I have authority to release You, and I have authority to crucify You?"
>
> Jesus answered, "You would have no authority over Me, unless it had been given you from above; for this reason he who delivered Me up to you has the greater sin." (John 19:7–11, NASB)

Jesus pointed out to Pilate what the centurion already knew: we do not possess authority; we are *under* it. He said that any authority we have has been given "from *above.*" It is revealing to observe that after this encounter, Pilate was actually intimidated by the rabble over which he supposedly had absolute authority. Fear had taken away all of the power he thought he had. He gave in to the will of the mob and turned Jesus over to them to be crucified. Like the Israelites before the giants or the disciples in the storm, he was controlled by fear. Fear reveals what we trust to secure our lives.

When Jesus first returned to His hometown to teach and heal, he was met with unbelief.

> "Where did this man get this wisdom and these mighty works? Is this not the carpenter's son?" So they were offended at Him. Now He did not do many mighty works there because of their unbelief. (Matthew 13:54b–55a, 57a, 58)

Failing to recognize Jesus' relationship with His heavenly Father, the source of all authority, these people could not see past his earthly father. They trusted perceived appearances rather than revealed truth.

We see yet another response confusing authority and power in Acts 8, this time involving a wizard. Philip was one of the first seven deacons chosen to serve in the congregation at Jerusalem. After the stoning of Stephen, another of these deacons, intense persecution started against the church in Jerusalem. The members were scattered throughout the region of Judea and Samaria, and they continued to proclaim the gospel. Philip went to Samaria teaching about Christ, healing the sick and lame, and casting out demons. In Samaria there was a man named Simon. He is described in Greek as a *magos*. It is the word from which the English word *magician* is derived. In this context, it refers to one who seeks out secret knowledge with which to manipulate people and events. He is described as using his sorcery to astonish the people, and he claimed to be someone great.

Many men and women believed the gospel, "and there was great joy in that city" (Acts 8:8). Simon himself believed the gospel of the kingdom of God and was even baptized. When the apostles in Jerusalem heard of the Samaritans receiving the gospel, they sent Peter and John to Samaria:

> . . . who when they had come down, prayed for them that they might receive the Holy Spirit. For as yet He had fallen upon none of them. They had only been baptized in the name of the Lord Jesus. Then they laid hands on them, and they received the Holy Spirit.
>
> And when Simon saw that through the laying on of the apostles' hands the Holy Spirit was given, he offered them money, saying, "Give me this power also, that anyone on whom I lay my hands may receive the Holy Spirit."
>
> But Peter said to him, "Your money perish with you, because you thought that the gift of God could be purchased with money! You have neither part not portion in this matter, for your heart is not right in the sight of God. Repent therefore of this your wickedness, and pray God if perhaps the thought of your heart may be forgiven you. For I see that you are poisoned by bitterness and bound by iniquity." (Acts 8:15–23)

Peter discerned Simon's motives and intents. His desire for power was fueled by bitterness. Bitterness describes deep resentment—usually coming from real or perceived victimization. We convince ourselves that we must control future relationships and experiences to guarantee that we will never be victims again. Being bound by iniquity (the Greek word, *adikias,* means injustice or unrighteousness) reveals that Simon was trying to control matters of his life himself and rejecting the authority of God. This same motive is all too prevalent even among believers today. This is why there are strong warnings about those entrusted with authority in the church, "lest being puffed up with pride he fall into the same condemnation of the devil" (1 Timothy 3:6). Of such a person we read:

> He is proud, knowing nothing, but is obsessed with disputes and arguments over words, from which come envy, strife,

> reviling, evil suspicions, useless wranglings of men of corrupt minds and destitute of the truth, who suppose that godliness is a means of gain. (1 Timothy 6:4–5a)

So then, we find many responses to the reality revealed by God. If we live our lives based on appearances, on what we perceive to be truth, fear will blind us to God and His provision. We will always be running from defeated giants, distracted by noisy storms, rejecting authority for the illusion of power, conforming to mediocrity, and ruled by fear. The alternative is trust in the King. Only then can we accept our helplessness in order to abide under God's authority. If we are not under the authority of God, we place ourselves in the power of whomever or whatever we fear. The illusion of personal control is just that: an illusion.

In light of these truths, the words of John Newton in his hymn "Amazing Grace" take on even more meaning: "'Twas grace that taught my heart to fear, and grace my fears relieved."

THE MYSTERY OF INIQUITY

"For the mystery of iniquity doth already work."
—2 Thessalonians 2:7, KJV

WHY IS IT SO DIFFICULT TO TRUST GOD? What prevents us from releasing the illusion of control?

We are born into this world with a human nature. The Bible calls this human nature the nature of the flesh. It is not to be confused with the body. The Greek word *sarx* is used to refer to flesh, while *soma* refers to the body. "Flesh" has to do with that which is of the earth as contrasted to that which is of heaven. It describes the aspects of life that are associated with survival on earth, with all the attendant desires, appetites, and limitations of that survival.

Our human nature was created by God to connect to Him, to live in intimate relationship with Him. It was not designed to live apart from this connection.

Flesh and Spirit

In Genesis 3, we find the tragic account of the separation of the first humans from God. To truly understand this event, we need to go back farther—to the rebellion of another created being who appears in the Genesis story as the serpent. This being was an angel entrusted with the highest authority of all the angels. He was named Lucifer (which means

"Day Star"). He is described as being beautiful and powerful. At some point before the creation of mankind, Lucifer became enamored with himself rather than his Creator. Isaiah records his intent:

> For you have said in your heart:
> "I will ascend into heaven,
> I will exalt my throne above the stars of God;
> I will also sit on the mount of the congregation
> On the farthest sides of the north;
> I will ascend above the heights of the clouds,
> I will be like the Most High."
> (Isaiah 14:13–14)

Each of these five declarations of "I will" represent responsibilities (and the control that goes with them) that belong to God alone. Only God is worthy to rule the hosts of heaven and the inhabitants of earth. In contrast to Lucifer's assertions, we find truth echoed throughout heaven and earth in Revelation:

> Then I looked and I heard the voice of many angels around the throne, the living creatures, and the elders; and the number of them was ten thousand times ten thousand, and thousands of thousands, saying with a loud voice:
> "Worthy is the Lamb who was slain
> To receive power and riches and wisdom,
> And strength and honor and glory and blessing!"
> And every creature which is in heaven and on the earth and under the earth and such as are in the sea, and all that are in them, I heard saying:
> "Blessing and honor and glory and power
> Be to Him who sits on the throne,
> And to the Lamb forever and ever!" (Revelation 5:11–13)

Now let us return to the garden in Genesis. This same Lucifer who chose to disconnect from God, the source of all life, has now come to the garden where God has placed the humans He created. "Garden of Eden" literally translates from Hebrew into "Garden of Delight," revealing the intention of God for us to find in Him the satisfaction of all desires and the source of joy.

> Delight yourself also in the Lord,
> And He shall give you the desires of your heart. (Psalm 37:4)

> You will show me the path of life;
> In your presence is fullness of joy;
> At your right hand are pleasures forevermore. (Psalm 16:11)

Lucifer is also known as the devil, or Satan (which means "the accuser"). Lucifer is now known by descriptions rather than a proper name, perhaps because in separating from God, he is no longer capable of relationship, only hunger—and a craving for the control to try to fill it.

The essence of the temptation of the humans consists of Satan deceiving them with the same lie he conceived: you can be your own god.

> And he said to the woman, "Has God indeed said, 'You shall not eat of every tree of the garden'?"
>
> And the woman said to the serpent, "We may eat the fruit of the trees of the garden; but of the fruit of the tree which is in the midst of the garden, God has said, 'You shall not eat it, nor shall you touch it, lest you die.'"
>
> Then the serpent said to the woman, "You will not surely die. For God knows that in the day you eat of it your eyes will be opened, and *you will be like God.*" (Genesis 3b–5a)

This lie was not confined to the garden—it is still being presented to us today. Satan proposes that if there is any control you don't have, then you are being deprived by God of something you need. The lie consists of two parts:

1) You cannot trust God to give you what you need.
2) You must be your own god and meet your own needs.

When the first humans chose to believe the lie, they too were separated from God. Now, not only had they rejected the nurture and security of intimate relationship with God, but they had placed themselves under the control of the usurper, Satan (2 Timothy 2:26 and 1 John 5:19, NIV).

In contrast, let us look at the temptation of Jesus by Satan in the wilderness. Jesus had gone without food for forty days.

> Now when the tempter came to Him, he said, "If you are the Son of God, command that these stones become bread." But [Jesus] answered and said, "It is written, 'Man shall not live by bread alone, but by every word that proceeds from the mouth of God.'" (Matthew 4:4)

The passage Jesus quotes here is Deuteronomy 8:3. In this passage, Moses is addressing the second generation of Israelites who were brought out of Egypt. He is reviewing the history of God's deliverance for the children of the Israelites who had been slaves in Egypt:

> And He humbled you, and let you be hungry, and fed you with manna that you did not know, nor did your fathers know, that He might make you understand that man does not live by bread alone, but man lives by everything that proceeds out of the mouth of the Lord. (Deuteronomy 8:3, NASB)

In essence, Jesus is saying, "I didn't come out here to feed myself, but to *be fed* by my Father. I came out here to experience hunger so that I might experience my Father's feeding me."

One of the best illustrations of the Genesis tragedy in the garden is in *The Lord of the Rings,* with J.R.R. Tolkien's description of the nine kings of men who were seduced by the dark lord.[8] The enemy offered them rings of power by which they could exercise more control. Only too late did they realize that by using these rings, they fell under the control of the dark lord who had made them. Rather than gaining more control, they lost all freedom and choice. They eventually became empty shells of men who did the bidding of their master. Just like the dark lord of the rings in Tolkien's story, our adversary shares his power with no one.

> Therefore, just as through one man sin entered the world, and death through sin, and thus death spread to all men, because all sinned . . . (Romans 5:12)

The Bible reveals that every human born since the rebellion in the garden (except for Jesus) is born with the consequences of that rebellion. We are born with a program in our hearts that directs us to be our own gods. This program is called "the sin nature" or "the flesh." The state of being controlled by this program is described as "walking in the flesh." The result of living under this program is slavery to the one who designed it. Like the kings in Tolkien's story, however, we may not realize this slavery as long as the illusion of control is maintained.

The Scriptures reveal that we don't become sinners by sinning—we sin because we have a sin nature (Romans 5:17–19; Romans 7:5, 8, 14–25; Romans 8:1–13; John 3:6; Ephesians 2:3; Galatians 5:17–21). The sin nature is not changed by changing our behavior. Rather, the change in our behavior results from God giving us a new nature.

We often underestimate the severity and complexity of the problem of sin; and in so doing fail to recognize the extraordinary scope and complexity of God's remedy. The Bible describes layers of consequences that came from the rebellion of Adam. These consequences involve our status before God, our relationship to God, and our fellowship with God.

There is a universal consequence that affects all creation, since Adam and Eve were given authority over creation on earth. In effect, they turned over the rule of earth to Satan (John 12:31, John 16:11, Ephesians 2:1–2). This choice violated the righteousness of God; and in separating from God, the source of life, also introduced death and suffering to all creation (Romans 8:19–23). They also doomed themselves and those who would come after them to be prisoners and slaves to Satan (2 Timothy 2:26). In addition, there is the consequence described earlier in which each human is born with a sin nature (Ephesians 2:3; Romans 7:5, 8, 14–25; Romans 8:1–13; John 3:6).

Beyond these truths, there is also an experiential consequence in which each of us acts out of this sin nature by believing lies and behaving in such a way as to be self-centered and control-seeking. We are controlled by our desires and fears and manipulated by our perceptions (Galatians 5:17–21). This is a state which the enemy hopes will blind us to God's remedy (Mathew 15:14; Mathew 23:16–26; John 12:39–40).

> But even if our gospel is veiled, it is veiled to those who are perishing,
> whose minds the god of this age has blinded, who do not believe,
> lest the light of the gospel of the glory of Christ, who is the image of
> God, should shine on them. (2 Corinthians 4:3–4)

The ultimate result of our sin problem is permanent alienation from God, which leaves us to share the fate of Satan just as we shared in his rebellion. This fate is unending, unimaginable torment that was not intended for humankind (Matthew 25:41, Revelation 20:10).

Regarding these truths, theologians use the terms *imputed*, *imparted* (or *transmitted*), and *personal* in describing both the sin problem and the divine solution. The word *impute* means to attribute or reckon something to a person.[9] Imputed sin is the legal consequence we suffer as a result of Adam's choice. His rebellion against God separated him from fellowship with God, who is righteous. We, as a result of imputed sin, are born unrighteous and also separated from fellowship with a righteous God. In His offer of salvation, Christ offers to have our imputed sin *imputed* to Him. That is, legally, He takes our debt as His own and pays it. He then *imputes* His righteousness to each believer who accepts His gift of salvation. We are considered righteous because of who He is and what He has done. This part of Christ's work changes our status before God.

> For if by the transgression of one, death reigned through the one, much more those who received the abundance of grace and the gift of righteousness will reign in life through the One, Jesus Christ.
>
> So then as through one transgression there resulted condemnation to all men, even so through one act of righteousness there resulted justification of life to all men.
>
> For as through the one man's disobedience the many were made sinners, even so through obedience of the One the many will be made righteous. (Romans 5:17–19, NASB)
>
> Giving thanks to the Father who has qualified us to be partakers of the inheritance of the saints in the light. He has delivered us from the power of darkness and conveyed us in the kingdom of the Son of His love, in whom we have redemption through His blood, the forgiveness of sins. (Colossians 1:12–14)

Another dimension of the problem (and solution) is that a sin nature is *imparted* or transmitted to us from this same ancestor, Adam. This is like inheriting a spiritual congenital defect that is terminal. That is, if not treated, this condition always results in spiritual death or permanent separation from God. This sin nature predisposes us to believe and live lies and to behave in accordance with our deception. The sin nature is ultimately self-centered as it attempts to be its own god. In this aspect, the sin nature reveals its source in reflecting the character of Satan. In effect, we proceed in word and deed to incur our own debt. This behavior, which theologians refer to as *personal sin,* is the experiential aspect of our sin problem and will be explored in more detail in chapter 7.

The solution for imparted sin, which Christ provides for those who receive His gift of salvation, is twofold. First, He substituted Himself in our place to condemn our sin nature on the cross. This means that He made it possible for our sin nature to be crucified with Him; in effect, to die with Him (Romans 8:1–13). He then, through His resurrection, caused us to be reborn in Him and then *imparted* to us a new nature, a spiritual nature, His Spirit living within us.[10] This aspect of Christ's work changes our relationship to God.

> And you were dead in your trespasses and sins, in which you formerly walked according to the course of this world, according to the prince of the power of the air, of the spirit that is now working in the sons of disobedience.
>
> Among them we too all formerly lived in the lusts of our flesh, indulging the desires of the flesh and of the mind, and were by nature children of wrath, even as the rest.
>
> But God, being rich in mercy, because of His great love with which He loved us, even when we were dead in our transgressions, made us alive together with Christ (by grace you have been saved), and raised us up with Him, and seated us with Him in the heavenly places, in Christ Jesus. (Ephesians 2:1–6, NASB)

> I have been crucified with Christ; it is no longer I who live, but Christ lives in me; and the life which I now live in the flesh I live by faith in the Son of God, who loved me and gave Himself for me. (Galatians 2:20)

If then you were raised with Christ, seek those things which are above, where Christ is, sitting at the right hand of God.

> Set your mind on things above, not on things on the earth.
> For you have died, and your life is hidden with Christ in God.
> When Christ who is our life appears, then you also will appear with Him in glory. (Colossians 3:1-4)

As believers who have received His gift, we not only enjoy eternal life with Christ, but also have the privilege of experiencing in this life this new nature and the truth and freedom it brings (John 3:16, John 10:10). Further, we can daily experience the forgiveness He made possible (1 John 1:9). How He helps us avoid identifying with the sin nature, and instead enjoy this new nature, will also be explored in chapter 7. This part of Christ's work changes our experiential fellowship with God.

When we take a casual attitude toward sin, we fall prey to two snares: we underestimate the power of sin to deceive and enslave us and we underestimate the power of grace to liberate us and keep us free.

Law and Grace

The word *law* has several meanings in the Scriptures. In a general sense, it refers to the revealed will of God.[13] It is most often used to refer to the written code of law given to Moses and intended for Israel, found in Exodus, Leviticus, and Deuteronomy.

After God miraculously brought the Israelites out of slavery in Egypt, He led them to Mount Sinai, where he gave the law to Moses. The law is made up of three parts: the moral law, the ceremonial law, and the civil law.

The civil law pertains to the ordering of the relationships and affairs of the people of Israel to each other; including real estate, property, and personal injury. The moral law, centering in the Ten Commandments, is an expression of God's holiness set against the sin problem in human nature. The ceremonial law pertains primarily to the system of sacrifices and offerings, anticipating the failure of the people to keep the moral law. Built into the law was the painful realization of our inability to keep it. What then was God's intent for the law?

> For I did not speak to your fathers, or command them in the day that I brought them out of the land of Egypt, concerning burnt offerings or sacrifices. But this is what I commanded them, saying, "Obey My voice, and I will be your God, and you shall be my people. And walk in all the ways that I have commanded you, that it may be well with you." Yet they did not obey or incline their ear, but followed the counsels and dictates of their evil hearts, and went backward and not forward. (Jeremiah 7:22–24)

The law was introduced because of sin. The problem God identified was not a performance problem, but a heart problem—trusting self rather than God.

The moral and ceremonial part of the law has two intentions. One intent is to separate God's people from the curse that corrupts the world—to set them apart as holy unto Himself. This section includes the kosher requirements in food and clothing. The second intent is to reveal the sin problem in the human heart and to anticipate the only remedy for that problem—the blood of the sacrifice.

> Therefore no one will be declared righteous in His sight by observing the law; rather, through the law we become conscious of sin. (Romans 3:20, NIV)

The law, therefore, is diagnostic, not prescriptive. It was intended to reveal a problem, not to solve it.

Notice the form in which the law is stated. When addressing behavior, the instruction is usually stated in negative form—prohibitions such as "thou shalt not." When the instruction is referring to belief, it is stated in the positive form, such as honoring father and mother, observing the Sabbath, "you shall love the Lord your God with all your heart" (Deuteronomy 6:5), and "fear the Lord" (Deuteronomy 6:2).

This pattern suggests that when one believes truth and trusts God, it creates an observable difference in behavior from those who do not. In contrast, if we see ourselves as behaving acceptably regardless of our heart attitude or intent, we end up deceiving ourselves like the Pharisees. It is far too easy to rationalize and justify our thoughts and beliefs as long as we create the appearance of righteousness in our outward behavior. It is possible to avoid the appearance of sin while trusting in self instead of God.

> For the Lord does not see as man sees; for man looks at the outward appearance, but the Lord looks at the heart. (1 Samuel 16:7b)

This is why Jesus was so angry with the Pharisees. They were thwarting the intent of the law, which was to expose sin and weakness so that the people would look to God to provide a solution. By twisting and amending the law with their man-made traditions, they effectively prevented it from exposing their fatal spiritual disease—sin. Thus blinded to their own disease, they saw no need for a cure, no need for the Messiah.

> Knowing this: that the law is not made for a righteous person, but for the lawless and insubordinate, for the ungodly and for sinners. (1 Timothy 1:9a)

Perhaps the reason for the negative injunctions of the law is that disease is usually diagnosed by the presence of a symptom—something that should *not* be there. If we observe in ourselves something that should not be there, we can then seek out the Great Physician.

If we were seeking a cancer screening, we would want the test to be as revealing as possible. How would we feel if we were told that the technician had set the sensitivity so that it would only reveal the really big tumors? When Jesus preached the Sermon on the Mount, he in effect recalibrated the law as a diagnostic tool so that it could once again reveal the condition of the heart.

> Do not think that I came to destroy the Law or the Prophets. I did not come to destroy but to fulfill.
>
> You have heard that it was said to those of old, "You shall not murder, and whoever murders will be in danger of the judgment."
>
> But I say unto you that whoever is angry with his brother without a cause shall be in danger of the judgment. And whoever says to his brother, "Raca!" [from the Hebrew word *rake,* meaning empty or worthless one] shall be in danger of the council. But whoever says, "You fool!" shall be in danger of hell fire.
>
> You have heard that it was said to those of old, "You shall not commit adultery."
>
> But I say to you that whoever looks at a woman to lust for her has already committed adultery with her in his heart. (Matthew 5:17, 21–22, 27–28)

Here we see a similar truth to the description of the *Logos* (Word) in Hebrews 4:12, where we are told it "is a discerner of the thoughts and intents of the heart." We shall explore this in more detail in chapter 7, where we discover Jesus Christ as the incarnate *Word* using the written Word of God to reveal what is in the heart.

Returning to our cancer analogy, how would we respond to the discovery of cancer in our body? Would we try to hide this cancer out of shame or fear? Would we get a knife and attempt to remove it ourselves? Would we be angry at the doctor for discovering it? No, rather, we would look to the physician for treatment. We would seek out and accept the cure that was offered.

Jesus said the law was summed up in two commandments, both stated in the positive: to love the Lord your God with all your heart and to love your neighbor as yourself.

> But now a righteousness from God, apart from the law, has been made known, to which the Law and the Prophets testify. This righteousness from God comes through faith in Jesus Christ to all who believe. (Romans 3:21–22a, NIV)

> For Christ is the end of the law for righteousness to everyone who believes. (Romans 10:4)

The solution for the problem revealed by the law is belief in Jesus Christ. He is described as the fulfillment of the law. The most commonly used Greek word for *iniquity* (*anomia)* is literally translated *lawlessness.* This refers to ignoring God's truth and following our own opinions and our own will, becoming a law unto ourselves.

The ultimate expression of this program of rebellion will be the "lawless one" described in 2 Thessalonians 2:8, who is the antichrist. His appearance and acceptance by most of the world will display the extent to which the spiritual blindness and deception of humankind will have grown. The Bible says that they will be deceived because they did not receive a love of the truth (2 Thessalonians 2:10). The chilling truth of this prophecy is that the ultimate consequence of ignoring the truth that is revealed to us is that we come to prefer lies to the truth. We choose to believe what feels most comfortable and what fits our lifestyle. Not only do we stop seeking truth, we stop desiring truth. We cannot recognize truth when we do not want truth.

> For the time will come when men will not put up with sound doctrine. Instead, to suit their own desires, they will gather around them a great number of teachers to say what their itching ears want to hear. They will turn their ears away from the truth and turn aside to myths. (2 Timothy 4:3–4, NIV)

Jesus is the fulfillment of all three parts of the law. Regarding the ceremonial law, He is the perfect and ultimate offering for sin—"the lamb of God who takes away the sin of the world" (John 1:29). He fulfills the sacrifices and intentions of the three prescribed annual feasts: the Feast of Unleavened Bread (Passover), the Feast of Weeks (Pentecost), and the celebration of the final harvest, called the Feast of Booths or Succoth (Deuteronomy 16:16).

First, He is the Passover lamb whose blood protects those under it from judgment (Exodus 12:22–27). He was slain on the eve of Passover outside the gates of Jerusalem (Deuteronomy 16:5–6), and He had just eaten the ritual Passover meal, or *seder,* with His disciples (Exodus 12:5–14). This Passover seder became "the Lord's Supper."

> Therefore purge out the old leaven, that you may be a new lump, since you truly are unleavened. For indeed Christ, our Passover was sacrificed for us. Therefore let us keep the feast, not with old leaven, nor with the leaven of malice and wickedness, but with the unleavened bread of sincerity and truth. (1 Corinthians 5:7–8)

Pentecost, from the Greek word meaning "fifty," was called the Feast of Weeks (Exodus 34:22), which refers to seven weeks (literally seven sevens) following the first day the grain was harvested. This first harvest was also called the firstfruits. Jesus sent His Holy Spirit to indwell believers on the first Pentecost following His resurrection (Acts 2:1–4, 41b), thus starting the church, the firstfruits of His harvest.

The Feast of Booths marks the final harvest. Prior to His return, Christ will gather all those who believe in Him to Himself—the final harvest (1 Thessalonians 4:16–17 and 1 Corinthians 15:52). He will then return and establish His kingdom on earth (Zechariah 14:16).

In addition to these three feasts, Jesus is also the fulfillment of most holy ritual prescribed by the law: the Day of Atonement, or Yom Kippur. Within the temple (and the tabernacle that preceded it) there was an inner chamber separated from the rest of the temple by a heavy veil or curtain (Exodus 26:31). This room was called the Holy of Holies or Most Holy. In this room was the ark of the covenant, which contained the tablets of the law given to Moses by God. Covering the ark was a lid called the mercy seat. In Exodus 25:22, God declared regarding the mercy seat, "There I will meet with you, and I will speak with you from above the mercy seat." No one was allowed to enter beyond this veil except one person on one day of each year. On the Day of Atonement, the high priest would enter behind this veil into the Holy of Holies and sprinkle the blood of the sacrifice on the mercy seat covering the ark of the covenant. The Hebrew word for atonement, *kawfar,* means "to cover" in the sense of satisfying a requirement, to cover sin, and to forgive.

The eyewitnesses of the crucifixion describe an amazing event immediately following the death of Jesus: "Then, behold, the veil of the temple was torn in two from top to bottom" (Matthew 27:51a). The veil of separation between God and mankind was torn from the top, showing an act of God, not an act of man. This veil was not just opened, it was torn, signifying that access to God was now permanent and this ritual would no longer need to be repeated. It occurred as the ultimate sacrifice had been accomplished: the death of the Lamb of God. In this scene we see Jesus Christ as both the sacrifice and the ultimate High Priest entering the presence of God, sprinkling His own blood on the mercy seat and securing our forgiveness. The Day of Atonement has come.

> But Christ came as High Priest of the good things to come, with the greater and more perfect tabernacle not made with hands, that is, not of this creation. Not with the blood of goats and calves, but with His own blood He entered the Most Holy Place once for all, having obtained eternal redemption. (Hebrews 9:11–12)

> But this Man, after He had offered one sacrifice for sins forever, sat down at the right hand of God . . . for by one offering He has perfected forever those who are being sanctified. (Hebrews 10:12, 14)

Along with the ceremonial law, Jesus is the fulfillment of the moral law:

> This is the covenant that I will make with them after those days, says the Lord: I will put my laws into their hearts, and in their minds I will write them. (Hebrews 10:16)

He alone can fulfill God's expectations of holiness and righteousness. We can, therefore satisfy the law by being joined to Christ and living in dependence upon Him.

> For what the law could not do in that it was weak through the flesh, God did by sending His own Son in the likeness of sinful flesh, on account of sin: He condemned sin in the flesh, that the righteous requirement of the law might be fulfilled in us who do not walk according to the flesh but according to the Spirit. (Romans 8:3–4)

In the book of Hebrews, we see how the law of Moses, the Torah, is fulfilled by Jesus Christ and the grace of God:

> For the Law is only a shadow of the good things that are coming—not the realities themselves. (Hebrews 10:1, NIV)

Throughout Hebrews, Jesus Christ is described as the ultimate high priest who completes all the sacrifices in heaven that were foreshadowed in the ceremonial law on earth. In the same way, the Sabbath, which is associated with rest, is shown to represent grace.

In the law, the Sabbath is patterned after God's resting upon the completion of His work of creation (Genesis 2:2–3). We find a parallel in Christ on the cross proclaiming, "It is finished!" (John 19:30). Here, He is declaring that the work of salvation is finished. We can experience this salvation by receiving it as a finished work. In this way, we enter into God's rest, ceasing from our own works as God did from His.

> For we also have had the gospel preached to us, just as they did; but the message they heard was of no value to them, because those who heard did not combine it with faith. Now we who have believed enter that rest . . .
>
> For if Joshua had given them rest, God would not have spoken later about another day. There remains, then, a Sabbath-rest for the people of God; for anyone who enters God's rest also rests from his own work, just as God did from His. Let us therefore make every effort to enter that rest so that no one will fall by following their example of disobedience. (Hebrews 4:2–3, 8–11, NIV)

This same word "fall" is used in reference to grace in Galatians:

> You who are trying to be justified by law have been alienated from Christ; you have fallen away from grace. (Galatians 5:4)

"Grace" refers to God's gift, God's initiative, God's love, and God's sufficiency directed toward us. As we experience God working in our lives, He trains us to trust Him. The more we grow to trust Him, the more we experience God working in our lives. Grace grows trust.

Some have been concerned that understanding grace in this biblical way leads to license or passivity. This indeed is the response of the flesh to the proposition of grace. The flesh says, "If I don't do it, it won't get done" or "God helps those who help themselves." The flesh has no frame of reference for motivation or accomplishment that is not the result of human effort or human motivation such as fear or obligation. The flesh cannot trust God, so it follows that the flesh cannot accept grace (Romans 8:7–8). How easy it is for activities like prayer, daily devotions, Bible reading, memorizing Scripture, church attendance, and witnessing to become ends in themselves; well-intentioned efforts to please God or satisfy some sense of duty. We fear God's disapproval if we fail in these duties. We think that the only alternative is self-indulgence, laziness, or passivity. In reality, the result of experiencing grace is the opposite of passivity. Paul says:

> But by the grace of God I am what I am, and His grace toward me was not in vain; but I labored more abundantly than they all, yet not I, but the grace of God which was with me. (1 Corinthians 15:10)

> For it is God who works in you both to will and to do for His good pleasure. (Philippians 2:13)

The one who has truly experienced the grace of God demonstrates a life of work and service, but this work is performed *by* God *through* the individual. It consists of experiencing God's promptings, God's energy, God's strength, God's wisdom, God's thoughts, God's love, and God's results. Who is glorified (revealed) by a life lived in this way?

> Whoever speaks, let him speak, as it were, the utterances of God; whoever serves, let him do so as by the strength which God supplies; so that in all things God may be glorified through Jesus Christ, to whom belongs the glory and dominion forever and ever. Amen. (1 Peter 4:11, NASB)

Finally, Christ also fulfills the civil law. This fulfillment is accomplished by the kingdom. As He establishes His authority and rule in the hearts of His people, the result is our loving one another as ourselves. Further, He will ultimately establish His kingdom literally over all rule and authority and remove all that clouds, obscures, and opposes truth. In that kingdom is completed love and perfect justice—no fear, no want, no oppression, no pain, no tears, and no death. In that kingdom is the restoration of all that the curse consumed. In that kingdom is joy forever in the presence of the King who loves us and made it all possible.

> *"He has delivered us from the power of darkness and conveyed us into the kingdom of the Son of His love."*—**Colossians 1:13**

THE MYSTERY OF CHRIST AND THE MYSTERY OF THE GOSPEL

". . . how that by revelation He made known to me the mystery (as I have briefly written already, by which when you read you may understand my knowledge in the mystery of Christ) . . . that the Gentiles should be fellow heirs, of the same body, and partakers of His promise in Christ through the gospel."—Ephesians 3:3–4, 6

"And for me, that I may open my mouth boldly to make known the mystery of the gospel."—Ephesians 6:19

"Now to him who is able to establish you by my gospel and the proclamation of Jesus Christ, according to the revelation of the mystery hidden for long ages past, but now revealed and made known through the prophetic writings, by the command of the eternal God, so that all nations might believe and obey him—to the only wise God be glory forever through Jesus Christ! Amen."—Romans 16:25, NIV

THE MOST PROFOUND TRUTH in the Bible concerns the identity of Jesus Christ. John, in the opening chapter of his gospel, writes:

> In the beginning was the Word, and the Word was with God, and the Word was God.
>
> He was in the beginning with God, all things were made through Him, and without Him nothing was made that was made.
>
> In Him was life, and life was the light of men. And the light shines in the darkness, and the darkness did not comprehend it. He came to His own and His own did not receive Him.
>
> But as many as received Him, to them He gave the right to become children of God, to those who believe in His name . . . And the Word became flesh and dwelt among us, and we beheld His glory, the glory as of the only begotten of the Father, full of grace and truth. (John 1:1–5; 11–12; 14)

Christ in the World

The Greek word used in John 1 for "Word" is *Logos*. It is that which was spoken by God. The Logos was in God and comes from God and is the expression of Himself. This Logos became flesh, that is, became a human being, so that He might carry out a plan to redeem mankind and all of creation. He became a human being so that He could communicate Himself to humankind. He became a human being so that He could die in our place. He then rose from the dead so that He could give us life with Him forever.

Jesus Himself, after His resurrection, appeared to two of His disciples while they were walking along the road to a village called Emmaus. He walked with them, but they did not recognize Him. They described their confusion and astonishment at the death of Jesus and the reports of His tomb being now empty. Jesus replied:

> "O foolish ones, and slow of heart to believe in all that the prophets have spoken! Ought not the Christ to have suffered these things and to enter into His glory?" And beginning at

> Moses and all the Prophets, He expounded to them in all the Scriptures the things concerning Himself. (Luke 24:25–27)

Here Jesus Himself discloses that He indeed is the one anticipated by the Scriptures. He is the one who was foreshadowed in the law and prophesied as the Messiah. He is presenting Himself as both fully man and fully God. As such, He is the only one who could do what He did for us. Further, as we saw in the opening Scripture of this chapter, He is making this salvation available not only to the Jews, but also to the Gentiles (which literally means "the nations").

The illusion of control that we explored in chapter 1 can take two forms. One form is believing we have direct control over whatever affects our life. The second form is believing we can manipulate whatever we think controls our life. For example, religions conceived by human nature usually involve some ritual or sacrifice by which a deity is manipulated to respond. In contrast, the Bible describes our relationship with God as *His* taking responsibility to make Himself known to us by *His* sacrifice. He aligns us with His will rather than us aligning Him with our will.

The Bible describes God's initiative to restore us to Himself as the *gospel,* or literally, the "good news." The good news involves God becoming human in the form of the prophesied Messiah, Jesus Christ. He is described as fully God and yet fully man. His name in Hebrew is: *Jeshua* (Savior), *Ha-meshia* (the Messiah, the Chosen or Anointed One). He came to reunite us to Himself for eternity, fulfilling His original intention in our creation. He accomplished this outcome by a multifaceted plan.

The Consequence of Rejecting God

In this plan, Jesus dealt with the consequence of our rejection of God, which is death. Since God is the only source of life, to separate from Him is death. The solution is resurrection. Christ died in our place so that we would not have to remain in a state of death or separation from God. He died in our place so that we would not have to remain in a state of slavery.

He rose from death and lives today so that we may know Him, and by being joined with Him, we are made alive. We are given the chance to share in His death so that we may share in His resurrection:

> Therefore we were buried with Him through baptism into death, that just as Christ was raised from the dead by the glory of the Father, even so we also should walk in newness of life.
>
> For if we have been united together in the likeness of His death, certainly we also shall be in the likeness of His resurrection, knowing this, that our old man was crucified with Him, that the body of sin might be done away with, that we should no longer be slaves of sin.
>
> For he who has died has been freed from sin.
>
> Now if we died with Christ, we believe that we shall also live with Him. (Romans 6: 4–8)

This death and resurrection begins in this life as a spiritual reality, but it will also be a physical reality. We are given the promise that after this physical body dies, we will one day experience a physical resurrection with a transformed body designed for eternal relationship with the One who loves us. To experience this restoration, we have only to believe this truth, rejecting the lie of being our own god.

The Consequence of the Sin Program

After dealing with our rejection of God, Jesus then dealt with the sin program that is still running in our lives. He accomplished this part of the plan by indwelling us. Since His resurrection, He desires to join with us in spirit. When we receive His gift of life, His Spirit enters us and remains with us for life. From within, He loves us, protects us, and transforms us into His image, undoing the damage that the sin program has done. Using the Scriptures, He displaces the lies with truth. As we are convinced of truth, we are set free from fear and anything that attempts to control us. This state of living with the indwelling Spirit of God is called the "spiritual nature." Jesus described this reality to one of the Jewish scholars, Nicodemus:

> Jesus answered and said to him, "Most assuredly, I say to you, unless one is born again, he cannot see the kingdom of God."
>
> Nicodemus said to Him, "How can a man be born when he is old? Can he enter a second time into his mother's womb and be born?"
>
> Jesus answered, "Most assuredly, I say to you, unless one is born of water and the Spirit, he cannot enter the kingdom of God. That which is born of the flesh is flesh, and that which is born of the Spirit is spirit. If I have told you earthly things and you do not believe, how will you believe if I tell you heavenly things? For God so loved the world that He gave His only begotten Son, that whoever believes in Him should not perish but have everlasting life. "For God did not send His Son into the world to condemn the world, but that the world through Him might be saved." (John 3:3–6, 12, 16–17)

Christ in the Believer: The Two Natures

As believers, the Bible tells us that we now have two natures: one born of flesh and one born of Spirit. As long as we occupy this body, we must deal with this reality. Recognition of these two natures is essential. Galatians 5:19–21 describes the "works of the flesh." These are the traits and inclinations of our fleshly human nature; the ultimate results of humans trying to be their own god:

Works of the Flesh

- *Adultery:* a violation of marital vows, involving a betrayal of trust. Being unfaithful. The emphasis is on the relationship—breaking *from* the relationship.

- *Fornication:* the root of this word is *porneo,* and it relates to prostitution; it is also the source of our word *pornography.* The emphasis is on the individual *joining to* an object of lust.
- *Impurity:* uncleanness. From the Greek word *akatharsia—a* means not, and *katharsia* (where we get the English word *catharsis*) means cleansed or purged. That which may not be brought into the presence of God. That which causes defilement. This word is also used to refer to impure motives and of unclean spirits.
- *Sensuality:* given over to and controlled by the desire for sensual stimulation. Unquenchable craving for sexual stimulation. Ruled by sexual desire.
- *Idolatry:* worship of false gods. The root combines *form* or *appearance* and *serve* or *worship.* To serve or worship that which appears to be god. God on our own terms.
- *Sorcery:* the root is *pharmakeuo,* which literally means to administer drugs. A practitioner of the magic arts; one who seeks to manipulate spiritual powers to his or her own ends. Attempting to find a substitute for God or attempting to manipulate God.
- *Hatred:* hostility, chronic bitterness. Controlled by resentment.
- *Strife:* a quarrel, contention. Oppositional. Conflict for the purpose of control.
- *Jealousy:* the root means "to boil." An envious and contentious rivalry. Insecurity. A consuming desire to possess.
- *Rages:* explosive anger, outbursts. Anger that overpowers its possessor.
- *Disputes:* the root means "to spin wool; a hireling." It is used of those who electioneer for office, courting popular applause by trickery and low arts. Partisan and factious spirit. Desire to put oneself forward. Selfish strife. Also used in Philippians 1:6, 2:3, 2 Corinthians 12:20, and James 3:14–16.
- *Dissensions:* divisions, conspiracy, seditions. Dissension for the purpose of drawing a following (contrast with "factions" below). Used in Romans 16:17 and 1 Corinthians 3:3.

- *Factions:* the root means "heresy." Dissensions arising from diversity of opinions and aims. Sects. Specifically, dissension arising from heresy. Used in 1 Corinthians 11:17–20, 2 Corinthians 6:17, and 2 Peter 2:1.
- *Envyings:* describes a state of dissatisfaction with what one has. "Painful or resentful awareness of the advantage enjoyed by another accompanied by a desire to possess the same advantage."[11]
- *Murders:* to slay. To take someone's life out of malice.
- *Drunkenness:* the root is from the word for "wine." Intoxication. Controlled by alcohol.
- *Carousings:* the root means "to lie outstretched." Revelings, overindulgence.

Fruit of the Spirit

In contrast, the next two verses, Galatians 5:22–23, describe the fruit of the Spirit. Notice that "fruit" is singular and not plural. We will explore the significance of this description later. These are the traits of the spiritual nature, the result of the Holy Spirit within the believer free and unhindered in revealing Christlikeness in and though us. The fruit of the Spirit is:

- *Love:* in the Greek, this is *agape,* sacrificial, unconditional love. Acceptance. Freedom from the fear of rejection. Agape love comes only from God (Romans 5:5). This love is unearned and undeserved. It does not depend on the response of the one being loved; therefore, we cannot lose it. It is the source of ultimate security, since there is no fear in this love (1 John 4:18). The entirety of chapter 13 of 1 Corinthians describes this agape love in detail. Agape can be fully experienced but not fully understood. Paul prays for the Ephesians that they be "rooted and grounded in love [*agape*]" and that they may "know the love of Christ which passes knowledge; that you may be filled with all the fullness of God" (Ephesians 3:17b, 19).

In the closing chapter of the gospel of John, Jesus, after His resurrection, has an intimate conversation with Simon Peter. He asks Peter three times, "Do you love me?" Peter is given the opportunity to affirm his love for Jesus three times after having denied knowing Him three times on the eve of the crucifixion. But there is more to this conversation.

In English we miss an important part of this communication. The Greek language has several different words for different kinds of love, all of which translate into English as *love.* The first two times Jesus asks the question, He is using a form of the word *agape.* Peter's response each time is to use a form of the word *phileo,* which means brotherly love or deep affection (the word from which we derive the name *Philadelphia,* meaning the city of brotherly love). *Phileo* is the highest form of love that a human can generate. However, Jesus was asking for something higher—agape. Peter was "grieved" when Jesus repeated the question a third time. He was offering to Jesus the best he could offer, just as he had done in Gethsemane on that painful night when in his zeal he cut off the ear of one of those sent to arrest Jesus. The same night when his strength failed and fear caused him to repeatedly deny that he knew Jesus. This third time, Jesus changed the word to *phileo,* and Peter's response was "Lord, You know all things; You know that I love [*phileo*] You" (John 21:17b).

This interaction was a continuation of the lesson Jesus had taught them from the beginning: what I am asking of you, you cannot give. I am the only source.

> He also presented Himself alive after His suffering by many infallible proofs, being seen by them during forty days and speaking of the things pertaining to the kingdom of God. And being assembled together with them, He commanded them not to depart from Jerusalem, but to wait for the promise of the Father . . .
>
> "For John truly baptized with water, but you shall be baptized with the Holy Spirit not many days from now . . . you

> shall receive power when the Holy Spirit has come upon you; and you shall be witnesses to Me in Jerusalem, and in all Judea and Samaria, and to the end of the earth." (Acts 1:3b–4a; 5, 8)

The unconditional agape love that Jesus asked of Peter can come only from His Spirit within us. This is why the instructions regarding husbands and wives and parents and children in Ephesians 5:22–6:4 come *after* the instruction to be filled with the Spirit (Ephesians 5:18) and the instruction to put off the fleshly nature and put on the spiritual nature (Ephesians 4:22–24). To attempt to apply the instructions regarding marriage and parenting without experientially learning to walk in dependence upon the Holy Spirit is utter futility.

The fruit of the Spirit continues:

- *Joy:* fullness, contentment, satisfaction. Various forms of the word *joy* are found almost two hundred times in the Scripture. It may be seen as the opposite of craving. Trust in God's sovereignty over provision.
- *Peace:* security. Freedom from fear. Protected. "And the peace of God, which surpasses all understanding, will guard your hearts and minds through Christ Jesus" (Philippians 4:7). Here is yet another of God's gifts that can be fully experienced but not fully understood. He makes it possible to enjoy peace even when the situation demands anxiety. Rest. Trusting in God's sovereignty over threats. Not the absence of conflict, but the presence of God.
- *Patience:* Living in God's time zone (which is eternity). Freedom from bondage to time. Tolerance. This word literally means "longsuffering." Trusting in God's sovereignty over circumstances. Endurance.
- *Kindness:* giving, caring. Freedom from self-concern. Generosity. Available for God to use.
- *Goodness:* reflecting light, not darkness. Righteousness.

- *Faith:* although some translations use *faithfulness,* the Greek word here is *pistis,* "faith." The ability to trust God. This ability to trust God makes us trustworthy. That is, as we trust God, others can trust us. Obedience. Courage. The result of God training our hearts to trust Him. This kind of faith cannot be generated by human effort or strength of will; it comes only from God: "Looking unto Jesus, the author and finisher of our faith" (Hebrews 12:2a). Experientially, it does not feel like holding on; it feels like being held. It is the heart's response to God's grace. It is the result of God purging us of the fear of everything but Him. It is the fear of the Lord.
- *Gentleness:* nothing to prove. Freedom to be vulnerable. Meekness. The human response to God's omnipotence.
- *Self-control:* this is not control *by* self; but control *of* self by Spirit. Empowering. God delegating control over ourselves to us. Freedom to choose. Freedom from addictions. Exercising dominion over self.

Notice the contrast between the *works* of the flesh and the *fruit* of the Spirit. We cannot produce the fruit of the Spirit. Everything on this list can come only from the Holy Spirit within us. The word *fruit* in Galatians 5 is singular rather than plural, which implies that the expression of the Holy Spirit in us is all or nothing. The believer is not strong in one trait and weak in another, for the fruit is not coming from the individual, but from the Holy Spirit.

We can receive and enjoy the fruit of the Spirit, but we cannot produce it. When we in our own efforts try to be spiritual, ultimately we produce only the works of the flesh. The results of our best efforts are but a poor and temporary counterfeit of God's fruit (Isaiah 64:6).

The War Within Us

Paul describes his personal experience of his two natures in Romans:

> For what I am doing, I do not understand. For what I will to

> do, that I do not practice; but what I hate, that I do. If, then, I do what I will not to do, I agree with the law that it is good. But now, it is no longer I who do it, but sin that dwells in me.
>
> For I know that in me (that is, in my flesh) nothing good dwells; for to will is present with me, but how to perform what is good I do not find. For the good that I will to do, do not do; but the evil I will not to do, that I practice.
>
> Now if I do what I will not to do, it is no longer I who do it; but sin that dwells in me. I find then a law, that evil is present with me, the one who wills to do good. For I delight in the law of God according to the inward man. But I see another law in my members, warring against the law of my mind, and bringing me into captivity to the law of sin which is in my members.
>
> O wretched man that I am! Who will deliver me from this body of death?
>
> I thank God—through Jesus Christ our Lord! So then, with the mind I myself serve the law of God, but with the flesh the law of sin.
>
> There is therefore now no condemnation to those who are in Christ Jesus, who do not walk according to the flesh, but according to the Spirit. (Romans 7:15–8:1)

These passages describe choices in everyday life. The term "walk" in these verses refers to the experience of living each day. The choice is between seeking to meet our needs and desires in our own efforts, limited by our own resources, or looking to the living God as our provider and protector in everyday life. Paul recognizes in himself two different natures. Three times in this one passage he distinguishes "I," which is Paul identifying himself with his new spiritual nature, and "sin" or "evil," which he recognizes as his fleshly nature. Even when he is aware of his fleshly nature, he does not identify with it: "Now if *I* do what *I* will not to do, it is no longer *I* who do it, but *sin* that dwells in me." He goes on in Romans 8 to instruct us to live "according to the Spirit" rather than "according to the flesh."

This word "according to" is a Greek preposition that can mean "after the manner of," "in the pattern of," "focused on," "agreeing with," "using," "based on," "within the limitations of," or "by means of." The phrase "set their minds" in Romans 8:5 is actually the verb form of the word "mind," which is "to mind." This word is synonymous with "to obey," showing us the connection with the earlier description in Romans 6:

> . . . knowing this, that our old self was crucified with Him, that our body of sin might be done away with, that we should no longer be slaves to sin; for he who has died is freed from sin.
>
> Now if we have died with Christ, we believe that we shall also live with Him, knowing that Christ, having been raised from the dead is never to die again; death no longer is master over Him. For the death that He died, He died to sin, once for all; but the life that He lives, He lives to God. Even so consider yourselves to be dead to sin, but alive to God in Christ Jesus.
>
> Therefore do not let sin reign in your mortal body that you should obey its lusts, and do not go on presenting the members of your body to sin as instruments of unrighteousness, but present yourselves to God as those alive from the dead, and your members as instruments of righteousness to God. For sin shall not be master over you, for you are not under law but under grace . . .
>
> Do you not know that when you present yourselves to someone as slaves for obedience, you are slaves of the one whom you obey, either of sin resulting in death, or of obedience resulting in righteousness? (Romans 6:6–14, 16, NASB)

Confusion has resulted from attempting to interpret the phrase "that our body of sin might be done away with" apart from the full context of this letter to the Romans. Some have erroneously interpreted this phrase to mean that "the body of sin" or fleshly nature has been removed so that we no longer have to deal with it. This interpretation would contradict the description in Romans 7:14–8:1 and the teaching of 1 John 1:8–2:2. These verses from 1 John begin with telling us that if we say we have no sin, we deceive ourselves; and they proceed to instruct us in how to experience ongoing forgiveness and cleansing through confession.

This phrase "done away with" is the Greek word *katargaythay*, meaning to "render powerless." It suggests the nullification of the rule of the flesh, the liberation of our wills to choose obedience to Christ. The image here is that of a king conquering an enemy who has been holding us prisoner and then setting us free to join this king. This is more evident in the parallel passage in Colossians:

> . . . having canceled the written code, with its regulations, that was against us and that stood opposed to us; he took it away, nailing it to the cross. And having disarmed the powers and authorities, he made a public spectacle of them, triumphing over them by the cross. (Colossians 2:14–15, NIV)

Returning to Romans 6:14 and 16, notice that we must choose to remain free. Our flesh is accustomed to slavery. Whenever we are faced with threat or pain, we tend to look to our old master and return to bondage. It is clear that there are only two options. If we reject the protection of the King, we will be recaptured by the enemy. If we daily choose submission to the King, we enjoy the riches of the kingdom.

> But seek first the kingdom of God and His righteousness, and all these things shall be added to you. (Matthew 6:33)

God's Grace

Some readers are confused by James's use of the term "works" in his epistle set in contrast to "faith," and they assume this to be a contradiction of Paul. Further reading, however, shows us that James uses *works* like Paul uses *fruit.* James describes works revealing true faith (James 2:18). Paul describes fruit revealing true faith. Peter uses *obedience* in the same way to describe our response to God's grace:

> Therefore gird up the loins of your mind, be sober, and rest your hope fully upon the grace that is to be brought to you at the revelation of Jesus Christ; as obedient children, not conforming yourselves to the former lusts, as in your ignorance; but as He who called you is holy, you also be holy in all your conduct, because it is written, "Be holy, for I am holy." (1 Peter 1:13–15)

Notice the sequence of grace bringing obedience, which in turn brings holiness. *Holiness* means being like God, set apart for Him—of the Spirit rather than of the earth. It is interesting to note that in the Greek, the instruction in verse 15, "you also be holy" is in imperative mood, which means a command, and passive voice, which means the action is being done *to* the subject, not *by* the subject. Therefore this command has the sense of "you also be made holy." Our holiness is from God, who is the only source of holiness. We can experience holiness because we are attached to the One who is holy. In his second letter, Peter says:

> Grace and peace be multiplied to you in the knowledge of God and of Jesus our Lord, as His divine power has given to us all things that pertain to life and godliness, through the knowledge of Him who called us by glory and virtue, by which have been given to us exceedingly great and precious promises, that through these you may be partakers of the divine nature, having escaped the corruption that is in the world through lust.

(2 Peter 1:2–4)

"Lust" in this passage means strong, consuming desire. "Corruption" relates to that which perishes (literally "rotting"). Here Peter is saying that we can escape a life of futility, emptiness, and death, consumed with our desires and needs, by experientially knowing God and believing His promises, which allows us to be joined to God and enjoy the fullness of His provision for all our needs in life.

Both James (James 4:6) and Peter (1 Peter 5:5–6) quote Proverbs 3:34: "God resists the proud but gives grace to the humble." Pride relates to self-sufficiency and an overinflated self-concept in which we try to be our own god. Humility refers to seeing ourselves as we truly are and seeing God as He truly is. In these passages, we see that true empowerment results from recognizing our own limitations and relating to God as He truly is.

Another source of confusion comes from a phrase used in Philippians 2:12: "*Work out* your own salvation with fear and trembling." To interpret this instruction accurately, let's look at the entire passage in context:

> So then, my beloved, just as you have always obeyed, not as in my presence only, but now much more in my absence, work out your salvation with fear and trembling; for it is God who is at work in you both to will and to work for His good pleasure. (Philippians 2:12–13, NASB)

Two different Greek words are used here: *energeo* (to work) and *katergadzomai* (to work out). *Energeo* is the direct exertion of energy, efficacy, and power. In the New Testament, it is usually used in relation to superhuman power and is never used to describe human effort. *Katergadzomai* means to bring forth as a result, to produce. "Work" describes the act, while "work out" describes the result. This is why we bring forth our salvation (the result of God's work) with fear and trembling. We are awed and overwhelmed by the beauty, the love, the power, and the tremendous cost of this gift.

This same word for "work out," katergadzomai, is used in some form six times in Romans 7: "But sin . . . *produced* in me all manner of evil desire (verse 8); "But sin . . . was *producing* death in me (verse 13); "For what I am *doing*, I do not understand" (verse 15); "But now, it is no longer I who *do* it, but sin that dwells in me" (verse 17); "But how to *perform* what is good I do not find (verse 18); "It is no longer I who *do* it, but sin that dwells in me" (verse 20). Katergadzomai is also used in 2 Corinthians 7:10: "For godly sorrow *produces* repentance leading to salvation, not to be regretted; but the sorrow of the world *produces* death."

Bringing together the insights of Romans 7 and Philippians 2, we find that indwelling sin produces (works out) evil and death, while the indwelling Christ produces (works out) righteousness and life.

In Ephesians 4:22–24, we discover something unexpected. When thinking of spiritual growth, we tend to expect our old nature (the flesh) to be removed or dealt with so that it no longer exists. We are consistently surprised when our fleshly nature manifests itself—"I thought I had overcome that." When we think of our spiritual nature, on the other hand, we expect it to be progressively improving, a work in progress—as if somehow we will receive in the future something we do not have now. In this passage, however, the opposite scenario is described. In describing the fleshly nature ("old self," NASB), the present tense is used: "it grows corrupt" or "is being corrupted [literally rotting] by deceitful desires." This tense describes present continuous action. When describing the spiritual nature ("new self"), the aorist tense is used, which describes action that started and was finished at a past point in time. In this case, the aorist tense means that the new spiritual nature was already created in the likeness of God "in true righteousness and holiness" *before we put in on.* It is a finished work, while freedom from the flesh is an ongoing, progressive experience. In this sense, spiritual growth may be seen not as adding something we don't already have, but as the removal over time of that which obscures and interferes with Christ in us.

Two Versions of the Fleshly Nature

There are two versions of the fleshly nature described in the Scriptures. The Corinthian Christians were struggling with fleshly nature that was hedonistic and ruled by appetites and desire. Paul addresses this problem with the Corinthians when he says,

> And I brethren, could not speak to you as to spiritual men, but as to men of flesh, as to babes in Christ . . . for you are still fleshly. For since there is jealousy and strife among you, are you not fleshly, and are you not walking like mere men? (1 Corinthians 3:1, 3, NASB)

Here, he is obviously talking to Christians who are living under the influence of the human (fleshly) nature, and as a result, they are indistinguishable from those who do not know God. He also points out that in this condition, they are more likely to identify with human leaders rather than God Himself:

> My brothers, some from Chloe's household have informed me that there are quarrels among you. What I mean is this: One of you says, "I follow Paul"; another, "I follow Apollos"; another, "I follow Cephas"; still another, "I follow Christ." Is Christ divided? Was Paul crucified for you? Were you baptized into the name of Paul? (1 Corinthians 1:11–13, NIV)

In sharp contrast, the Galatian Christians revealed another form of the fleshly human nature: they were trying to be more righteous by human effort. They were trying to keep the law by their own strength and understanding in order to be acceptable to God.

> You foolish Galatians! Who has bewitched you? Before your very eyes Jesus Christ was clearly portrayed as crucified.

> I would like to learn just one thing from you: did you receive the Spirit by observing the law, or by believing what you heard? Are you so foolish? After beginning with the Spirit, are you now trying to attain your goal by human effort? (Galatians 3:1–3, NIV)

Our human nature can be not only hedonistic but also religious. In this form we may even, with good intentions, attempt to please God in our own efforts. We may pray, tithe, attend church, attempt to share the gospel, and help the needy.

A woman in her early fifties became extremely distraught and sought help. She had grown up in the church. She even worked at the regional office of the denomination. She had attended church regularly with her children. She could not understand why God had allowed her husband to leave and eventually divorce her. She could not understand why her children had turned against her. Over time, she came to accept the truth. She had been performing for her husband and thought she could perform for God. She failed to understand the depth and depravity of her unsaved husband. He had infected the family and her life with his sin. She did not truly know how to relate to God.

A man was best known for always being present when the church doors were open. He tried to please the pastor by doing odd jobs without charge. He was once overheard fussing and complaining about how much was expected of him. His service became a burden to him, rather than a joy.

If we are not trusting God and living in dependence upon Him, all this activity is no different from any other man-made religion. It serves only to glorify the individual rather than God. We can often recognize the results of the flesh trying to be spiritual when we pursue education and Christian service only to discover in the midst of ministry that we have become cynical, bitter, or disillusioned.

In the gospel of Luke we find Jesus in the village of Bethany teaching in the home of two sisters, Mary and Martha. Mary was sitting at the feet of Jesus, listening and learning. Martha was feeling responsible for preparing food and serving all her guests. At one point, Martha had had enough.

> But Martha was distracted with much serving, and she approached Him [Jesus] and said, "Lord, do You not care that my sister has left me to serve alone? Therefore tell her to help me."
>
> And Jesus answered and said to her, "Martha, Martha, you are worried and troubled about many things. But one thing is needed, and Mary has chosen that good part, which will not be taken away from her. (Luke 10:40–42)

It always struck me as odd that Martha thought it was her job to feed the man who had fed the five thousand on the hillside. This scene is replayed frequently in churches today. We sacrifice and work hard, thinking we are serving God. Sooner or later there is the recognition that we are overworked and unappreciated. We may, like Martha, begin to complain to God and even presume to tell Him what He ought to do to remedy this situation. An alternate form of the same problem may be telling others what they ought to be doing. A third option is to form a committee.

Our fleshly nature may try to be spiritual through self-sacrifice or self-discipline. We may attempt to restrict or conform ourselves to some standard of thought or behavior. This attempt at becoming Christlike from the outside in is a substitute for the Holy Spirit growing us into Christlikeness from the inside out.

> Therefore do not let anyone judge you by what you eat or drink, or with regard to a religious festival, a New Moon celebration or a Sabbath day. These are a shadow of the things that were to come; the reality, however, is found in Christ. Do not let anyone who delights in false humility

> and the worship of angels disqualify you for the prize. Such a person goes into great detail about what he has seen, and his unspiritual mind puffs him up with idle notions. He has lost connection with the Head, from whom the whole body, supported and held together by its ligaments and sinews, grows as God causes it to grow.
>
> Since you died with Christ to the basic principles of this world, why, as though you still belonged to it, do you submit to its rules: "Do not handle! Do not taste! Do not touch!"? These are all destined to perish with use, because they are based on human commands and teachings. Such regulations indeed have an appearance of wisdom, with their self-imposed worship, their false humility and their harsh treatment of the body, but they lack any value in restraining sensual indulgence. (Colossians 2:16–23, NIV)

In the next chapter of Colossians, we find a parallel passage to Ephesians 4:22–24 in which Paul instructs us in the alternative to self-restraint and self-improvement. This alternative is to:

> . . . put to death whatever belongs to your earthly nature . . . since you have taken off your old self with its practices and have put on the new self, which is being renewed in knowledge in the image of its Creator. (Colossians 3:5a, 9b–10, NIV)

In the third chapter of Corinthians dealing with the contrast between the spiritual nature and the fleshly nature, Paul writes:

> . . . you are God's building. According to the grace of God which was given to me, as a wise master builder I have laid the foundation, and another builds on it. But let each take heed how he builds on it. For no other foundation

> can anyone lay than that which is laid, which is Jesus Christ.
>
> Now if anyone builds on this foundation with gold, silver, precious stones, wood, hay, straw, each one's work will become clear; for the Day will declare it, because it will be revealed by fire; and the fire will test each one's work, of what sort it is.
>
> If anyone's work which he has built on it endures, he will receive a reward. If anyone's work is burned, he will suffer loss; but he himself will be saved, yet so as through fire. (1 Corinthians 3:9b–15)

Here we see that even well-intentioned works can be performed in the flesh. Human motives and human resources, like the human nature itself, are limited and temporary. The works produced by human natures are like those natures, temporary and limited in quality and effectiveness by the limited minds that made them. In contrast, works that are done through us by the Holy Spirit will be, like Him, eternal and of a quality that reflects the mind and hand of God. The results of works done in the flesh glorify the human who did them. The results of works done in the Spirit glorify God. In Philippians chapter 4, Paul declares:

> I can do all things through Him who strengthens me. (Philippians 4:13, NASB)

Paul teaches this same truth that we first explored in Ephesians 4:22–24 in all of his letters to the churches:

> Not that we are adequate in ourselves to consider anything as coming from ourselves, but our adequacy is from God, who also made us adequate as servants of a new covenant, not of the letter, but of the Spirit; for the letter kills, but the Spirit gives life. (2 Corinthians 3:5–6, NASB)

> And for this purpose also I labor, striving according to His power, which mightily works within me. (Colossians 1:29, NASB)

> But by the grace of God I am what I am, and His grace toward me was not in vain; but I labored more abundantly than they all, yet not I, but the grace of God which was with me. (1 Corinthians 15:10)

> But we have this treasure in earthen vessels, that the excellence of the power may be of God and not of us. (2 Corinthians 4:7)

> I have been crucified with Christ; and it is no longer I who live, but Christ lives in me; and the life which I now live in the flesh I live by faith in the Son of God, who loved me and delivered Himself up for me. (Galatians 2:20, NASB)

> Now may the God of peace Himself sanctify you completely; and may your whole spirit, soul, and body be preserved blameless at the coming of our Lord Jesus Christ. (1 Thessalonians 5:23)

> But the Lord is faithful, who will establish you and guard you from the evil one. (2 Thessalonians 3:3)

Paul, toward the end of his letter to the Romans, instructs us to:

Present your bodies a living and holy sacrifice, acceptable to God, which is your spiritual service of worship. And do not be conformed to this world, but be transformed by the renewing of your mind. (Romans 12:1b–2a)

In contrast to our performing, we are instructed to present ourselves as a sacrifice. This word implies an animal that is being sacrificed, which is bound and helpless on the altar. The word "conformed" is in the middle voice in Greek, which expresses action being done by the subject to itself: "Do not conform yourself to this world." The Greek word for "transformed" is *metamorphousthay,* from which we derive *metamorphosis.* It is in the passive voice, in which the action is being done to the subject, not by the subject: "Be transformed." "Renewing," *anakainosis,* is a noun that implies a replacement of something old with something new. In this case, replacing lies with truth. When this word is used as a verb in the Scriptures, as in Colossians 3:10, it is also in the passive voice. The word used in Ephesians 4:23, *ananeoo,* "be renewed," is also in the passive voice. Correlating these Scriptures, we see that the individual is responsible for the problem (being conformed to the world); while God is responsible for the solution (being transformed). The message that consistently echoes throughout the New Testament is that God is offering to do a work in the believer.

How does God accomplish this transformation in the believer? If we cannot achieve godliness by our effort and dedication, how then does it happen? How do we recognize when God is doing this work in us? This is the mystery of godliness.

THE MYSTERY OF GODLINESS

"But if I am delayed, I write so that you may know how you ought to conduct yourself in the house of God, which is the church of the living God, the pillar and ground of the truth.

And without controversy great is the mystery of godliness:
God was manifested in the flesh,
Justified in the Spirit,
Seen by angels,
Preached among the Gentiles,
Believed on in the world,
Received up in glory."
—1 Timothy 3:15–16

HOW CAN WE DISCERN THE SPIRITUAL NATURE from the fleshly nature? How can we recognize truth from deception, reality from appearance? One way of distinguishing these differences is by looking at the manifestations of these two natures as described in Galatians 5:19–23. We can recognize the deeds of the flesh and the fruit of the Spirit in both ourselves and others. In this, we are not judging people; we are inspecting fruit. We are looking for congruity between words and behavior, between beliefs and choices.

Judgment: God's Method for Revealing Truth in Us and to Us

The challenge before us is recognizing what to trust within ourselves, as well as who and what to trust from others in our lives. God's method for revealing truth is the same in either situation. In the same chapter where we are admonished to "judge not that you be not judged" (Matthew 7:1), we are also instructed to beware of false prophets:

> You will know them by their fruits. Do men gather grapes from thorn bushes or figs from thistles? Even so, every good tree bears good fruit, but a bad tree bears bad fruit.
>
> A good tree cannot bear bad fruit, nor can a bad tree bear good fruit . . . Therefore by their fruits you will know them. (Matthew 7:16–18, 20)
>
> Either make the tree good and its fruit good, or else make the tree bad and its fruit bad; for a tree is known by its fruit. (Matthew 12:33)

If it looks like a duck, walks like a duck, and quacks like a duck, it is probably not an eagle—even if it claims to be one.

> Brethren, join in following my example, and note those who so walk, as you have us for a pattern. For many walk, of whom I have told you often, and now tell you even weeping, that they are enemies of the cross of Christ: whose end is destruction, whose god is their belly, and whose glory is in their shame—who set their mind on earthly things. (Philippians 3:17–19)

Who to Believe? Who to Follow?

The context of these passages involves spiritual leadership. The principle of fruit inspection is given to us for the purpose of deciding who to believe and who to follow. God intended this instruction to be used for protecting the believer. Keep in mind that these principles apply both to ourselves and to others. Daily we are challenged to recognize within ourselves which nature we are operating out of; in a sense, who to believe and who to follow even within our own minds and hearts.

The Greek word for "to judge" is *krino.* A *kritays* is a judge. *Krisis,* the root of our English word *crisis,* is judgment. The root of all these words is *kri,* which means "to separate" in the sense of distinguishing one thing from another. In the Scriptures, we are told that only the Judge is authorized to judge (judging belongs in God's circle). We are, however, instructed to *discern* (*dia-krino,* with the literal meaning "to judge through") and to examine or *appraise* (*ana-krino,* with the literal meaning "to judge again"). Both terms imply that we are recognizing what the Judge has already judged. Discernment suggests "seeing through," or recognizing the difference between things that God has exposed or revealed. It is used of distinguishing between good and evil, flesh and spirit. It is also used in reference to detecting motive and intent. Appraisal is used in reference to examining and recognizing value, worth, or origin, distinguishing that which is genuine from the counterfeit.

> But a natural man does not accept the things of the Spirit of God; for they are foolishness to him, and he cannot understand them, because they are spiritually *appraised.* But he who is spiritual *appraises* all things, yet he himself is *appraised* by no man. (1 Corinthians 2:14–15, NASB)

> But to me it is a very small thing that I should be *examined* by you, or by any human court; in fact, I do not even *examine* myself. I am conscious of nothing against myself, yet I am not by this acquitted; but the one who *examines* me is the Lord.

> Therefore do not go on passing *judgment* [krino] before the time, but wait until the Lord comes, who will both bring to light the things hidden in the darkness and disclose the motives of men's hearts; and then each man's praise will come to him from God. (1 Corinthians 4:3–5, NASB)

> But if we *judged* [dia-krino, "discerned"] ourselves rightly, we should not be *judged* [krino]. But when we are *judged* [krino], we are disciplined by the Lord in order that we may not be *condemned* [*kata-krino,* "to judge against"] along with the world. (1 Corinthians 11:31–32, NASB)

This sort of judgment is an essential part of the Christian life. We are instructed to exercise discernment regarding prophetic utterances (1 Corinthians 14:29), to discern spirits (1 Corinthians 12:10), and to discern good and evil (Hebrews 5:14).

Testing

Discernment and appraisal each describe a *process* of recognizing truth and error, good and evil. The *methods* used to reveal truth and error or good and evil are described by two Greek words for *testing. Dokimadzete* means to prove by testing. It describes a positive test intended to reveal the presence of something. In some contexts it can be compared to a litmus test, in which a treated strip of paper changes color when exposed to certain chemicals. In other contexts it resembles a smelting or refining furnace in which metals such as gold or silver are purified by burning off impurities or by causing separation of the precious metal from the ore in which it is embedded. The Scriptures describe this kind of test being performed both by God and by believers, depending on the context. This word is translated with a variety of English words and is shown in the following passages in italics:

It is used in *proving* (in the sense of confirming) the will of God

(Romans 12:2, Ephesians 5:10), to *test* each person's work (1 Corinthians 3:13, Galatians 6:4), to *examine* ourselves in preparation for the Lord's Supper (in the sense of discovering and removing impurities, 1 Corinthians 11:28), and to *test* the spirits (1 John 4:1); it is "the *proof* of your faith . . . *refined* by fire" (1 Peter 1:7); it is both words used in "We have been *approved* by God to be entrusted with the gospel . . . God, who *examines* our hearts" (1 Thessalonians 2:4), and "*Test* everything" (1 Thessalonians 5:21).

The instrument of testing is described in Hebrews:

> For the word of God is living and powerful, and sharper than any two-edged sword, piercing even to the division of soul and spirit, and of joints and marrow, and is a *discerner* of the thoughts and intents of the heart. (Hebrews 4:12)

The Greek word for "discerner" is *kritikos,* which means "capable of distinguishing." The "word of God" in this passage is *logos,* the same word used in the opening verses of the gospel of John which we examined in chapter 3. *Logos* describes that which God has spoken, whether in creation, when He spoke the world into existence, in the inspired Scriptures (2 Timothy 3:16), or in the Word becoming flesh in Jesus Christ.

The use of *logos* here signifies more than our attempting to use the Bible as a topical reference guide for decision making. It means that we are to submit our minds and hearts to the Incarnate Word (Jesus Christ) while we examine the written Word (the Bible). The Holy Spirit interprets and applies the written Word to our minds and hearts to reveal truth about us and about Him. He can separate and reveal the beliefs and intents of our two natures ("soul and spirit" in Hebrews 4:12 correspond to flesh and spirit as we have discussed them in this book). It would be impossible for us to recognize these natures on our own.

The second word for test is *pyradzete,* which in most contexts is a negative test intended to reveal the absence of something. It is usually translated as "tempt" and is not from God (Matthew 4:1, 6:13; Hebrews 4:15;

James 1:2, 13; 1 Peter 4:12; 2 Peter 2:9; and Revelation 3:10). Even in these passages, however, we find that God uses these tests, in spite of the intent of the tempter, to accomplish His own intentions.

Testing for the believer, then, is the result of exposing anything to the purifying presence of the Spirit of God. Whether this test results from us bringing ourselves or a teaching into His presence or from Satan attempting to deceive us, both will be used by God for His loving intention of liberating us from bondage and fulfilling His plan of redemption in which all things will be restored (Romans 8:20–23). We are again reminded of Joseph's declaration to his brothers that what they intended for evil, God used for good (Genesis 50:20).

Deception

Since our adversary's primary weapon against us is deception, it is obvious that discernment is essential for living in this world. How do we acquire discernment? The Bible reveals a twofold source: the Scriptures and the Holy Spirit.

> But solid food is for the mature, who because of practice have their senses *trained* to discern good and evil. (Hebrews 5:14)

God's method of maturing us involves training us to discern by practice. "Solid food" refers to the teaching of the Scriptures. "Senses" is translated from a Greek word that describes an "organ of discernment" that we possess in Christ. The word for "trained" in this passage is a form of *gymnadzo,* from which we get our word *gymnasium.* The passage implies an Olympic athlete being coached to master a skill or ability by repetitive practice. The athlete knows that he or she must submit himself or herself to a coach for this process. The athlete also knows that this training will be painful.

Judgment, then, is not synonymous with condemnation. Condemnation is the consequence of resisting or ignoring judgment. Judgment is intended to reveal truth. This intent is evident even in the function of the Jewish priests of the Old Testament:

> And they [the priests] shall teach my people the difference between the holy and the unholy, and cause them to discern between the unclean and the clean. (Ezekiel 44:23)

This kind of judgment takes place here and now. Since the purpose of judgment is to separate, we are most likely to recognize judgment by the presence of conflict. Flesh opposes Spirit, and Spirit opposes flesh (Galatians 5:17). This conflict can be within the individual (Romans 7:15–8:1), between people in a church (1 Corinthians 11:18–19), or between believers and unbelievers in the world (John 15:18–19). The distinguishing feature that sets this kind of conflict apart as judgment is that it results from the revelation or exposure of truth.

Errors in Handling Scripture

When we explored the deeds of the flesh listed in Galatians 5:19–21, we encountered the word *factions.* This is from the Greek word *hairesis,* from which we derive the English word *heresies.* Hairesis literally means "a choice or opinion." In the biblical context, it describes an opinion that is not based on true interpretation of the Scriptures and discernment. Theologians use the term *exegesis* to describe the biblical method or process of interpreting the Scriptures. Exegesis means to bring meaning out of Scripture, as opposed to *eisegesis,* which attempts to read into Scripture one's own ideas.

Paul in 2 Corinthians describes many who were "peddling the word of God" in contrast to the sincerity of him and his companions (2 Corinthians 2:17). In chapter 4, he describes this contrast further by stating that he and his companions do not "handle the Word of God deceitfully" (2 Corinthians 4:2). The Greek word used is a form of *dolos,* which means *decoy* or *bait.* This word implies an intent to trap or capture, whether the intent is human and intentional or demonic and making use of oblivious human instruments.

Instruction on Interpretation of Scripture

Peter describes judgment applied to those teaching heresies in the context of giving us instruction on interpretation of Scripture.

> But know this first of all, that no prophecy of Scripture is a matter of one's own interpretation, for no prophecy was ever made by an act of human will, but men moved by the Holy Spirit spoke from God. But false prophets also arose among the people, just as there will also be false teachers among you, who will secretly introduce destructive heresies, even denying the Master who bought them, bringing swift destruction upon themselves. And many will follow their sensuality, and because of them the way of the truth will be maligned;
>
> And in their greed they will exploit you with false words; their judgment from long ago is not idle, and their destruction is not asleep. (2 Peter 1:20–2:3, NASB)

Near the end of his letter, Peter points out another source of error in mishandling Scripture:

> . . . and regard the patience of our Lord as salvation; just as also our beloved brother Paul, according to the wisdom given him, wrote to you, as also in all his letters, speaking in them of these things, in which are some things hard to understand, which the untaught and unstable distort, as they do also the rest of the Scriptures, to their own destruction.
>
> You therefore, beloved, knowing this beforehand, be on your guard so that you are not carried away by the error of unprincipled men

> and fall from your own steadfastness, but grow in the grace and knowledge of our Lord and Savior Jesus Christ. To Him be the glory, both now and to the day of eternity. Amen. (2 Peter 3:15–18, NASB)

In contrast to those who mishandle the Word of God, Paul instructs Timothy to be diligent to rightly divide or handle accurately the word of truth (2 Timothy 2:15). The word in the Greek for "rightly divide" is *orthotomeo*, which means "to cut a straight line." The implication is to have a guide, pattern, or straightedge to cut with, or in an agricultural sense, to have a marker to sight with across a field in order to plow a straight line. In addition, in the next chapter of his letter, Paul says:

> You, however, continue in the things you have learned and become convinced of, knowing from whom you have learned them; and that from childhood you have known the sacred writings which are able to give you the wisdom that leads to salvation through faith which is in Christ Jesus.
>
> All Scripture is inspired by God and profitable for teaching, for reproof, for correction, for training in righteousness; that the man of God may be adequate, equipped for every good work. (2 Timothy 3:14–17, NASB)

Submitting Our Minds and Hearts to the Holy Spirit

In order to accurately interpret the Bible, we need to submit our minds and hearts to the Holy Spirit so that He may disclose and correct the thoughts and intents of the heart. Like Jesus on the road to Emmaus with the two disciples, the Spirit will also open our minds to understand the Scriptures, for they are spiritually discerned. In addition, we need to learn to study the meaning of the words of Scripture in grammatical and historical context and correlate the individual passages with the whole of the Bible in order to bring meaning out rather than read opinions into the Scripture. Further, we are admonished to have a pattern to cut with, which indicates a way of comparing the meaning we bring out both with the Bible as a whole and with what trustworthy teachers who have gone before have taught. We can look to the fruit of the lives of these teachers to see evidence of the Holy Spirit.

If truth from God is revealed to an individual, that person's flesh will resist and oppose it. The biblical instruction is to crucify the flesh in Christ. If that is accomplished, the believer is free to walk in the Spirit. If the flesh is indulged, then the Spirit will confront this believer continuously. This experience has often been described as being under conviction.

If truth from God is revealed to a church or other group of believers, those who are walking in the flesh will find themselves resisting the one or ones who present it. If those in leadership are walking in the Spirit and exercising discernment, those who are opposing the truth will either come under conviction in order to recognize and accept truth or they will leave the fellowship. If the leadership is walking in the flesh, then those through whom the truth was revealed may choose to leave (1 Timothy 6:3–5).

In 1 Corinthians 5:1–12, we see an example of a believer under judgment within the church. This individual persisted in immorality. The rest of the congregation not only failed to stand on truth so that he might be confronted with the danger of his situation, but they even accepted and supported his behavior. The result was that this sin spread like a disease and infected the church (2 Timothy 2:17–18). The others in the church became arrogant. Perhaps they were proud of the magnitude of their tolerance, or their pride was due to their following human leaders rather than God (1 Corinthians 1:10–13). At any rate, Paul warned them of the danger of this spiritual infection and pointed out that the desired response of the church was not pride, but instead, grief.

This pride can manifest in the church today in two extremes: judging in the place of God rather than discerning (Romans 14:10–13) on the one hand, and inappropriate tolerance in which we trust our own minds rather than discerning the mind of Christ on the other. This is the same pattern revealed earlier between the overindulgent version of the fleshly nature and the religious version of the fleshly nature. When we are walking in intimate communion with Jesus, we not only have access to the mind of Christ (1 Corinthians 2:16), but we also feel His feelings. He is grieved by sin (Ephesians 4:30, Mark 3:5), and so we feel the pain of his grief.

Paul's response to this crisis was to instruct the church to "deliver such a one to Satan for the destruction of his flesh, that his spirit may be saved in the day of the Lord Jesus" (1 Corinthians 5:5, NASB). This is similar to what happened to Ananias and his wife, Sapphira, when their sin threatened to infect the church in Jerusalem (Acts 5:1–11). They sold some land and announced to the church that they were giving all the proceeds of the sale to the church. They then conspired to keep some of the money while attempting to create the false impression that they were as generous as others who had previously been prompted by the Holy Spirit to sell land in order to help those in need in the church. They lied to the church, but more importantly, Peter discerned that they had allowed Satan access to their hearts and that he had convinced them to lie to the Holy Spirit. If we were to judge from outward appearances, this incident would appear to be simply a self-centered act intended to impress people. When Peter used discernment, however, a satanic infection of the body of Christ (the church) was disclosed. Peter's words were, "Why has Satan filled your heart to lie to the Holy Spirit?" The focus here is not merely on the motives of Ananias, but on the intent of Satan. Remember that this rebuke is coming from Peter, one who knows all too well how it feels to have Satan attempt to play out his intentions in our weaknesses. Earlier in Peter's life we see him attempting with good intentions to argue with Jesus as Peter tries to prevent Him from going to His death. The response of Jesus is very revealing:

> But He turned and said to Peter, "Get behind Me, Satan! You are an offense to Me, for you are not mindful of the things of God, but the things of men."(Matthew 16:22-23)

Later on, Peter again experienced the influence of Satan as Satan "sifted him as wheat"; resulting in Peter's threefold denial of Christ on the night of Jesus' arrest. (Luke 22:31–32).

Judgment for Ananias and Sapphira took the form of physical death. Paul observes in the Corinthian church that because they have partaken of communion in "an unworthy manner," that is, indulging the fleshly nature, many among them are weak, sick, or dead (1 Corinthians 11:27–30). Partaking in "an unworthy manner" is contrasted with the instruction of Christ to "do this in remembrance of Me" (1 Corinthians 11:24-25); and in verse 29 is further described as "not discerning the Lord's body". In verse 34, Paul instructs them to satisfy their hunger at home so that they do not "come together for judgment". Correlating these scriptures leads us to recognize a contrast between setting our minds on our own desires as opposed to setting our minds on Jesus. Colossians 3:2 mirrors this same truth in saying, "Set your mind on things above, not on things on the earth". It is in this context that he admonishes them:

> But if we judged ourselves rightly, we should not be judged. But when we are judged, we are disciplined by the Lord in order that we may not be condemned along with the world.
> (1 Corinthians 11:31–32, NASB)

Here we see God's contingency plans (Plan A and Plan B, if you will) to train us to recognize truth and protect us from deception. If we learn discernment through God's training (Plan A), we can enjoy discovering truth—the truth that sets us free. If we resist or ignore God's efforts to train us in discernment, then He must resort to confrontation through discipline (Plan B). This discipline is motivated by love and is a privilege reserved only for God's children (Hebrews 12:5–11). The end result of both plans is the same: that believers will recognize and act on truth.

What was the outcome of Paul's intervention in the church at Corinth?

> For I wrote you out of great distress and anguish of heart and with many tears, not to grieve you but to let you know the depth of my love for you. If anyone has caused grief he has not so much grieved me as he has grieved all of you, to some extent—not to put it too severely. The punishment inflicted on him by the majority is sufficient for him. Now instead, you ought to forgive and comfort him, so that he will not be overwhelmed by excessive sorrow. I urge you, therefore, to reaffirm your love for him. The reason I wrote you was to see if you would stand the test and be obedient in everything. If you forgive anyone, I also forgive him. And what I have forgiven—if there was anything to forgive—I have forgiven in the sight of Christ for your sake, in order that Satan might not outwit us. For we are not unaware of his schemes. (2 Corinthians 2:4–11, NIV)

The intervention by Paul, motivated by love, accomplished its purpose: the believer in error was set free from his bondage. He returned to the church with the experiential knowledge of truth, the church was delivered from the trap of pride (trust of self) and learned to obey God, and forgiveness was enjoyed by all. In addition, with the exposing of the satanic trap, those in the church were now educated and less likely to be caught themselves. God had been glorified in the eyes of the church and the watching world.

It is sobering to realize the responsibility and danger involved in ministry to the body of Christ and the crucial role of discernment in growing and protecting believers. It is for this reason that James warns believers:

> Let not many of you become teachers, my brethren, knowing that as such we shall incur a stricter judgment. (James 3:1, NASB)

The most important truth emerging from these accounts is that we are to exercise discernment rather than relying on appearances, trusting the Holy Spirit rather than our own perceptions. I recall a few years ago, looking in the mirror and seeing on my face what looked like an insignificant mole, a small blemish. After ignoring it for months, I finally went to a dermatologist, who biopsied this mole and determined it was a malignant skin cancer. It had to be surgically removed, and thankfully, none of the cancer remained. Paul uses the same analogy when instructing Timothy regarding those who were teaching heresy, describing their teaching as spreading like gangrene or cancer (2 Timothy 2:17).

Unity in the Church

God's method of bringing unity to the church is not by making unity an end in itself. Unity results when the individual believers submit to the Holy Spirit and seek His will rather than their own (Ephesians 4:3, 13). Unity is the fruit of believers walking in the Spirit—being of one Spirit.

> It was he who gave some to be apostles, some to be prophets, some to be evangelists, and some to be pastors and teachers, to prepare God's people for works of service, so that the body of Christ may be built up until we all reach unity in the faith and in the knowledge of the Son of God and become mature, attaining to the whole measure of the fullness of Christ.
>
> Then we will no longer be infants, tossed back and forth by the waves, and blown here and there by every wind of teaching and by the cunning and craftiness of men in their deceitful scheming. Instead, speaking the truth in love, we will in all things grow up into Him who is the Head, that is, Christ. From him the whole body, joined and held together by every supporting ligament, grows and builds itself up in love, as each part does its work. (Ephesians 4:11–16, NIV)

Churches have split over the differences between the truth of the

Spirit and the lies of the flesh. Dr. Charles Stanley of First Baptist Church of Atlanta tells the story of his early days in the pulpit at this church. During the Sunday morning worship service as he was preaching, a church member of an opposition faction left his seat and accosted Dr. Stanley with a physical punch. Dr. Stanley continued to preach each week; while that faction soon left the church.[12]

Notice that this kind of conflict usually does not originate from the one with the truth, as if he or she were fighting for a cause. Rather, the pattern of the conflict within judgment is such that those opposing truth attack, while those with truth resist and stand (Ephesians 6:13–14).

> But avoid foolish and ignorant disputes, knowing that they generate strife. And a servant of the Lord must not quarrel but be gentle to all, able to teach, patient, in humility correcting those who are in opposition, if God perhaps will grant them repentance so that they may know the truth, and that they may come to their senses and escape the snare of the devil, having been taken captive by him to do his will.
>
> But know this, that in the last days perilous times will come: for men will be lovers of themselves, lovers of money, boasters, proud, blasphemers, disobedient to parents, unthankful, unholy, unloving, unforgiving, slanderers, without self-control, brutal, despisers of good, traitors, headstrong, haughty, lovers of pleasure rather than lovers of God, having a form of godliness but denying its power. And from such people turn away! (2 Timothy 2:23–3:5)

There is a sequence involved in judgment. First, within each believer, God seeks to separate the fleshly nature from the spiritual nature. Then, within the church, God separates those walking in the Spirit from those relying upon the flesh (whether believers choosing to live in their flesh or unbelievers who, out of ignorance or malicious intent, infiltrate the church).

> Now the Spirit expressly says that in latter times some will depart from the faith, giving heed to deceiving spirits and doctrines of demons, speaking lies in hypocrisy, having there own conscience seared with a hot iron. (1 Timothy 4:1–2)

> For the time has come for judgment to begin at the house of God; and if it begins with us first, what will be the end of those who do not obey the gospel of God? (1 Peter 4:17)

Finally, judgment comes upon the world as the purified church is separated from the fallen world system that lies under the power of the Evil One. In this way, those who walk in darkness may clearly see "a great light" (Isaiah 9:2). This separation is also a form of conflict that usually takes the form of persecution (2 Thessalonians 1:4–5).

Historically, we can see this sequence as a cycle of reformation. In the fourteenth century, John Wycliffe of England and John Huss of Bohemia rediscovered the truths of grace that had been buried under encrusted traditions of the empty religion of the Dark Ages. Wycliffe translated the Scriptures from Latin to English so that the common people might read for themselves and enter into personal relationship with God. Wycliffe (c. 1330–1384) wrote:

> Some worldly folk puffed up with learning treat Scripture lightly and irreverently, despising its logic and style; they are like the gentiles who thought Christ a fool for his humility and patience. But the faithful whom he calls in meekness and humility of heart, whether they be clergy or laity, male or female, bending the neck of their inner man to the logic and style of Scripture will find in it the power to labour and the wisdom hidden from the proud.[13]

In the sixteenth century, Martin Luther and other European Reformers, along with another generation of English Reformers including

Thomas Cramner and William Tyndale, rediscovered these same truths and also created translations of Scripture in the languages of the common people. Cramner was burned at the stake, and Tyndale, whose English translation served as the foundation of the King James Version, was tortured and executed.

Martin Luther, like the other Reformers, looked to the Scriptures alone as the ultimate authority for and source of truth. In light of this belief, he translated the Bible into German to make it accessible to individual believers. He taught that salvation was by grace, not works. When put on trial for his teachings, he declared, "On this I take my *stand*. I can do no other. God help me. Amen."[14]

Perhaps the most disturbing observation in these atrocities is that the persecution is coming from those who call themselves "the church." This is the result of failing to "rightly divide the word of truth" (2 Timothy 2:15), and failing to seek and accept God's purifying judgment of His church. The reality revealed by the Scriptures is that Satan seeks to infiltrate and control the church so that he may suppress truth and replace God on earth. Consistent with the intent revealed in his rebellion (Isaiah 14:12–14), Satan seeks to rule in heaven and on earth. We who abide under the authority of the King, our Lord Jesus, are instructed to *stand* in Satan's way (Ephesians 6:11–18). We see the ultimate expression of this strategy in the role of the "false prophet" who will arise in the end times during the Great Tribulation as one who "worked signs in his [the beast's] presence, by which he deceived those who received the mark of the beast and those who worshipped his image" (Revelation 13:11–15; 19:20).

Throughout history, those with teachable hearts who were submitted and responsive to God took their stand on truth that He revealed. Persecution followed. And the cycle continues: by the seventeenth century, there was already a need to purify that which had been reformed, so we see the rise of the Puritans and the Separatists who sought to rediscover the truths of grace uncovered by the Reformers.

In the historic Bodleian Library of Oxford University, I was reading an eighteenth-century history of the English church. This book recounted the story of the early Reformers, followed by that of the Puritans and the Separatists. At the end of this book is a single line in Latin: *"Ecclesia semper reformanda."*

A very proper British librarian informed me that this was a motto of the Reformation and translated as "The church always reforming." This means that each generation of believers must seek out the Lord and test for truth in what we believe and what we are taught. If we attempt in a secondhand manner to rely upon the traditions of those who learned how to walk with God, we will inevitably be drawn into self-reliance and drift further into empty, man-made religion. Each denomination and every generation runs this risk.

> For judgment I am come into this world, that they which see not might see; and they which see may be made blind. (John 9:39)

> Therefore the Lord said:
> "Inasmuch as these people draw near with their mouths
> And honor Me with their lips,
> But have removed their hearts far from Me,
> And their fear toward Me is taught by the commandment
> of men,
> Therefore, behold, I will again do a marvelous work
> Among this people,
> A marvelous work and a wonder;
> For the wisdom of their wise men shall perish,
> And the understanding of their prudent men shall be hidden."
> (Isaiah 29:13–14)

The Furnace of Affliction: God's Method for Growing Us in Truth

> I have tested you in the furnace of affliction. (Isaiah 48:10b)

> The refining pot is for silver and the furnace for gold, but the Lord tests the hearts. (Proverbs 17:3)

> For You, O God, have tested us;
> You have refined us as silver is refined . . .
> We went through fire and through water;
> But You brought us out to rich fulfillment. (Psalm 66:10, 12b)

A wise teacher once asked his class, "How do we grow spiritually?"

The responses focused on the familiar disciplines of the faith: prayer, Bible study, fellowship, church attendance, and service. The teacher then challenged the students to do another study, but this time making it biographical rather than topical. The students set out to research the lives of biblical men and women who were used of God, including patriarchs, prophets, and disciples. The result was the observation that one common feature of all the individuals studied was suffering. This was the furnace of affliction, the refining fire.

Reality of Helplessness

As we observed in chapter 2, what makes these experiences opportunities for growth is the very reality of helplessness. In the book of Daniel, there is an account of three of Daniel's friends, brought with him as exiles from Judah to Babylon. After refusing to worship the gods of Babylon, they were thrown into a furnace by the order of the king.

> And these three men, Shadrach, Meshach, and Abed-Nego, fell down bound into the midst of the burning fiery furnace.

> Then King Nebuchadnezzar was astonished; and he rose in haste and spoke, saying to his counselors, "Did we not cast three men bound into the midst of the fire?" They answered and said to the king, "True, O king."

> "Look!" he answered, "I see four men loose, walking in the midst of the fire; and they are not hurt, and the form of the fourth is like the Son of God." (Daniel 3:23–25)

Let us notice two truths in this marvelous passage. The first is that the only thing that was burned by the fire was the ropes that bound the men. This furnace, intended by their captors to destroy them, was used by God to set them free. Secondly, they met Jesus in the furnace. We may infer that He was waiting for them there—in the furnace. How often we pray and sing about growing closer to the Lord. What if His answer to this prayer takes the form of a furnace opening before us and Jesus within bidding us to enter? Indeed, this is the biblical pattern for intimacy with God. This is how He conforms us to His image and completes His purpose for our lives.

> Therefore since Christ suffered for us in the flesh, arm yourselves also with the same mind, for he who has suffered in the flesh has ceased from sin, that he should no longer live the rest of his time in the flesh for the lusts of men, but for the will of God . . .
>
> Beloved, do not think it strange concerning the fiery trial which is to try you, as though some strange thing happened to you; but rejoice to the extent that you partake of Christ's sufferings, that when His glory is revealed, you may also be glad with exceeding joy. (1 Peter 4:1–2, 12–13)
>
> And after you have suffered for a little, the God of all grace, who called you to His eternal glory in Christ, will Himself perfect, confirm, strengthen and establish you. (1 Peter 5:10, NASB)

Growth through Suffering

In this passage, Peter reassures us that suffering does not mean that something has gone wrong or that we have failed somehow. Instead, he confirms that this is the normal Christian life: suffering is God's method for growing us, freeing us from fear, and securing our joy and our peace. Through it, He trains us to align our circles and let Him be God. Helplessness is the portal to grace. We cannot truly experience the grace of God without passing through the experience of helplessness. David describes this experience so beautifully in the most familiar Psalm in the Bible:

> Yea, though I walk through the valley of the shadow of death, I will fear no evil; For you are with me; Your rod and your staff, they comfort me. (Psalm 23:4)

Here, David describes a situation in which it is too dark to see the path. The shadow of death is impenetrable darkness. He cannot see the Shepherd. He cannot hear the Shepherd. But he can feel the presence of the Shepherd as the Shepherd gently touches him with rod and staff to guide his steps.

If we always needed to see where we were going, then we could easily be misdirected by our enemy; for we would be depending on our vision. If we always needed to hear His voice, we would be confused when we were deafened by the din of the world and the raging battle around us; for we would then be depending on our understanding.

> Trust in the Lord with all your heart,
> And lean not on your own understanding;
> In all your ways acknowledge Him,
> And He shall direct your paths.
> (Proverbs 3:5–6)

With college graduation just a few months away, I found myself experiencing "senior panic," that anxiety that grips us when we realize that we are now leaving the predictable world of school and venturing into the unknown real world. My friend and prayer partner, Rick Brawner, and I decided to spend a day in prayer to seek God's direction. We went to a nearby state park and trekked to opposite sides of the lake. The lake was frozen over, and a powdery snow was falling. I was struck by the stillness and the quietness of this beautiful place.

For the next few hours, I prayed and searched the Scriptures for answers. I employed every technique I had ever been taught about discovering God's will: a pro-con list, searching for biblical examples, laying out a "fleece" (from Gideon), and even random opening of the Bible like a Magic 8 Ball. As the sun began to set, I was colder but no closer to finding direction. At about that time, the quietness was broken by a loud quack echoing over the surface of the frozen lake. These quacks continued until curiosity drove me to seek out the source. Around the bend in the lake, I discovered a large white duck swimming in circles in a hole in the ice. Upon seeing me, he quacked even more excitedly, clambered up onto the ice, and made his way to the bank where I was standing. I offered him some crackers I had in my coat pocket, and he nibbled up every crumb. As he looked expectantly at me, I said, "Sorry, that's all I've got."

Since it was getting darker, I began making my way back along the shore. When I looked back, the duck, still down on the ice, was doing his best to follow me. I couldn't take him back to the dorm, and I didn't want to leave him stranded on the ice. I looked out over the lake and noticed a patch of open water where a stream was flowing into the lake. *I've got it,* I thought. *If I walk toward the stream, the duck will follow me; and I can lead him right into the open water.* I headed for the stream, and the duck, waddling on the ice, wouldn't take his eyes off me. He wasn't watching where he was going, he was watching me. Before long, the ice was getting thinner under him, and he finally broke through, plunging into the water near the mouth of the stream. He shook the water off his tail, looked around, and with a parting quack, paddled off up the stream.

With darkness setting in, I started off for the parking lot when the realization hit me. It was as if God said, "Hear the parable of the duck. Fix your eyes on Me and follow Me just like the duck followed you. You don't have to know where to go next. Trust Me to direct you."

Once again, in the Scriptures and in life, God reminds us that He will take responsibility for us. Prayer, Bible study, fellowship, worship, witnessing, and service are descriptive rather than prescriptive in the life of a believer. That is, when we are experiencing grace as a way of life, God stimulates in us a hunger for His Word, a longing for true fellowship, and a desire to worship Him, commune with Him (both listening and speaking), and share Him with others. We find our greatest joy in His pleasure.

During my seminary years, in a dark and neglected nursing home in New Orleans, I met a truly godly woman who introduced herself as "Miss Rosey." She had never married and had outlived all her close relatives. She was suffering the effects of unmanaged diabetes and had lost one leg, most of the fingers of one hand, and most of the sight in both eyes. She was alone and helpless in the most depressing place I had ever visited. My friend Tim Cochran and I originally went to this place to minister to the residents, yet she quickly turned the tables and each Sunday would minister to us. She was full of the joy of the Lord, and she would always lead us in worship as she sang beautiful spirituals and gospel hymns a capella like only someone born and raised in New Orleans could. Later, we would sit at her feet and she would impart wisdom to us.

On one Sunday, she said, "You boys are over at the seminary, and you are going to make a preacher" (this was a phrase from my grandparents' generation which meant, "You are preparing for ministry"). She continued, "You will hear many smart men, educated men. But listen especially close to the ones that have been through the fire. You can tell the ones that have been through the fire—because when they speak, you can *smell* the smoke!"

Miss Rosey was right.

> On a certain day, Jesus and his disciples came upon a man born blind.
>
> And His disciples asked Him, saying, "Rabbi, who sinned, this man or his parents, that he was born blind?" Jesus answered,

> "Neither this man nor his parents sinned, but that the works of God should be revealed in him." (John 9:1–3)

God's Intention in our Suffering

When we ask why, we tend to look to the past to find the origin of a problem. But when Jesus answers the why, he looks to the intention of God for the present and the future—what He has lovingly planned to accomplish with this problem. God would have us look to the outcome He performs, not the circumstances that created the problem. He invites us to rest in His control and His love.

When Lazarus became ill, his sisters Mary and Martha sent word to Jesus:

> "Lord, behold, he whom you love is sick."
>
> When Jesus heard that, he said, "This sickness is not unto death, but for the glory of God, that the Son of God may be glorified through it" . . . So when He heard that he was sick, He stayed two more days in the place where He was. (John 11:3–4, 6)

Even though Lazarus died, Jesus revealed that the purpose of this sickness was not death, but the glory of God. When Jesus finally arrived, Martha and Mary both told Him that if He had been there, Lazarus would not have died. Jesus answered Martha, "Your brother will rise again" (John 11:23).

Martha's response was a theological one: "I know that he will rise again in the resurrection at the last day" (John 11:24).

Martha, like many of us when pierced with grief at the death of a loved one, found little comfort in a promise of a distant future hope. But Jesus brought this promise to present reality when He said to her,

> I am the resurrection and the life. He who believes in Me, though he may die, he shall live. And whoever lives and believes in Me shall never die. Do you believe this? (John 11:25–26)

In answer, Martha confessed her belief that Jesus was the Christ, the Son of God. Yet, when Jesus instructed them to open the tomb shortly afterward, she objected that there would be a stench since Lazarus had been dead for four days. Once again, we can see in her the correct theology but faltering faith.

> Jesus said to her, "Did I not say to you that if you would believe you would see the glory of God?" (John 11:40)

What followed was Jesus fulfilling God's purpose for the death of Lazarus—resurrection. In allowing this event, He revealed a remarkable truth to Martha and all those present: being joined to Jesus is life. The believer who dies passes from life unto life. Death is experienced only by those who observe.

> But I do not want you to be ignorant, brethren, concerning those who have fallen asleep, lest you sorrow as others who have no hope. For if we believe that Jesus died and rose again, even so God will bring with Him those who sleep in Jesus. (1 Thessalonians 4:13–14)

Lazarus and his sisters were not the only believers to experience the purpose of God in their trials. At the Last Supper, Jesus disclosed to Peter that he was about to experience a trial:

> And the Lord said, "Simon, Simon! Indeed, Satan has asked for you, that he may sift you as wheat. But I have prayed for you, that your faith should not fail; and when you have returned to Me, strengthen your brethren."
>
> But he said to Him, "Lord, I am ready to go with You, both to prison and to death."
>
> Then He said, "I tell you, Peter, the rooster shall not crow this day before you will deny three times that you know Me." (Luke 22:31–34)

Here is a parallel to the opening scene in the story of Job: Satan accusing and seeking permission from God to afflict a believer. The satanic intention was most likely to have two disciples committing suicide that night, Judas and Peter. God, however, used Satan for His intention: to empty Peter of Peter so that he could be filled with the Spirit fifty days later at Pentecost. This same Peter on that day, filled with the Holy Spirit, proclaimed the gospel—and three thousand people received the gift of salvation.

In the closing chapter of 1 Corinthians, Paul wrote that he would remain in Ephesus longer than planned because God had opened a great door for effective ministry, *and* there were many adversaries. This capital of the province of Asia was renowned for the temple of the goddess Artemis (or Diana), which was one of the seven wonders of the ancient world, and for being the center of the occult in the ancient world. After hearing the gospel, the practitioners of the occult made bonfires of their occult books. So many people came to believe in Christ that the silversmiths, whose livelihood depended on selling statues of the goddess, were going bankrupt and rioted.

Yet here in the midst of this effective ministry, Paul was still being purified:

> We do not want you to be uninformed, brothers, about the hardships we suffered in the province of Asia. We were under great pressure, far beyond our ability to endure, so that we despaired even of life. Indeed, in our hearts we felt the sentence of death. But this happened that we might not rely on ourselves but on God, who raises the dead. (2 Corinthians 1:8–9, NIV)

By allowing this experience, God trained Paul and his companions not to trust in themselves. Further, He took them beyond trusting Him to prevent death—like Martha, He took them to trusting Him to raise the dead. The last vestige of fear has been burned away. The flesh has been crucified; Satan has been disarmed.

> Later in the same letter, Paul described "a thorn in my flesh, a messenger of Satan, to torment me" (2 Corinthians 12:7 NIV). This "thorn" is believed to be some condition in his body that caused pain or disability. He prayed three times for God to remove it, but instead God said, "My grace is sufficient for you, for my power is made perfect in weakness" (verse 9). Paul's response reveals the paradox of the life of the believer:
>
> That is why, for Christ's sake, I delight in weaknesses, in insults, in hardships, in persecutions, in difficulties. For when I am weak, then I am strong. (2 Corinthians 12:10 NIV)

Peter echoes the same truth in his epistle where we are once again reminded of the mystery of God transforming our will into His will:

> Therefore, since Christ suffered for us in the flesh, arm yourselves also with the same mind, for he who has suffered in the flesh has ceased from sin, that he no longer should live the rest of his time in the flesh for the lusts of men, but for the will of God." (1 Peter 4:1–2)

In his letter to the Philippians, Paul discloses the *secret* of contentment:

> I know how to get along with humble means, and I also know how to live in prosperity; in any and every circumstance I have learned the secret of being filled and going hungry, both of having abundance and suffering need. I can do all things through Him who strengthens me." (Philippians 4:12–13, NASB)

Perhaps the secret of contentment lies in the answer to the question, "Do you believe that you and I can conceive of a life better than the one

God has designed for us?" If not, we can accept God's method of growing us spiritually and trust His intent. We no longer have to fear the furnace if we are convinced Jesus Himself is waiting for us within it—to set us free from that which binds us so that we can embrace Him and grow deeper in intimacy with Him. We cannot experience God's strength until we first experience our own weakness. Truly, the furnace of affliction is the portal to grace.

NINE

THE MYSTERY IS FINISHED

"But in the days of the voice of the seventh angel, when he is about to sound, then the mystery of God is finished, as He preached to His servants the prophets."—Revelation 10:7, NASB

"And to make all see what is the fellowship of the mystery, which from the beginning of the ages has been hidden in God who created all things through Jesus Christ; to the intent that now the manifold wisdom of God might be made known by the church to the principalities and powers in the heavenly places, according to the eternal purpose which He accomplished in Christ Jesus our Lord."—Ephesians 3:9–11

"Then comes the end, when He delivers the kingdom to God the Father, when He puts an end to all rule and all authority and power. For He must reign till He has put all enemies under His feet. The last enemy that will be destroyed is death."—1 Corinthians 15:24–26

IT IS IMPORTANT TO REALIZE that when God allows a furnace experience in our lives, His intent transcends our individual lives. As we have seen, God uses the experiences of our lives, particularly the ones marked by our helplessness, to free us from fear, transform us into His likeness, and deepen our intimacy with Him. But there is more.

The Fellowship of the Mystery: We Are Not Alone

Once we receive His gift and indwelling Spirit, we become a part of something far greater than ourselves: we become a part of the living body of Christ—the church—that fellowship of true believers who live in dependence upon Him. These believers who have been refined in the furnace become colonies of the kingdom, those who seek the rule of the King in their hearts—anticipating the return of the King and ultimately reigning with Him in His kingdom. We are then privileged to participate in the completion of the miracle of redemption, both on earth and in the spiritual realm.

Creation and the Believer

> For I consider that the sufferings of this present time are not worthy to be compared with the glory which shall be revealed in us. For the earnest expectation of the creation eagerly waits for the revealing of the sons of God.
>
> For the creation was subjected to futility, not willingly, but because of Him who subjected it in hope; because the creation itself will also be delivered from the bondage of corruption into the glorious liberty of the children of God. For we know that the whole creation groans and labors with birth pangs until now.
>
> Not only that, but we also who have the firstfruits of the Spirit, even we ourselves groan within ourselves, eagerly waiting for the adoption, the redemption of our body. (Romans 8:18–23)

Since the creation—all living things created by God on earth—was subjected to the curse as a result of the rebellion of the first Adam, so the creation will be set free from the curse by the obedience of the second Adam, who is Christ. The animals and living things on earth had been placed under the authority of Adam at creation. Their fate was forever joined to his. The angels that sinned were immortal beings. Angels did not desire, nor did God offer them, a recourse for salvation. When these angels rebelled, they were destined to remain in that state of rebellion and condemnation until the final judgment. Humans who rebelled incurred physical death as part of their judgment. That is why after they rebelled, God stationed an angel to block their access to the Tree of Life in the garden of Eden. He ensured they could not eat of it in their fallen state and become as the fallen angels (demons) are—doomed to a state of permanent alienation from God (Genesis 3:22–24). In a twist only the divine could conceive, God has used the physical death that was part of the curse to become the means whereby Christ could redeem us by suffering physical death in our place and allowing us to join in His resurrection. This resurrection culminates with our receiving a new body like Christ's.

> So also is the resurrection of the dead. The body is sown in corruption, it is raised in incorruption. It is sown in dishonor, it is raised in glory. It is sown in weakness, it is raised in power. It is sown a natural body, it is raised a spiritual body. And as we have borne the image of the man of dust, we shall also bear the image of the heavenly Man.
>
> Behold, I tell you a mystery: We shall not all sleep, but we shall all be changed—so when this corruptible has put on incorruption, and this mortal has put on immortality, then shall be brought to pass the saying that is written: "Death is swallowed up in victory."
>
> "O Death, where is your sting?
> O Hades [grave], where is your victory?"

> The sting of death is sin, and the strength of sin is the law. But thanks be to God, who gives us the victory through our Lord Jesus Christ. (1 Corinthians 15:42–44a, 49, 51, 54–55)

Embedded in this marvelous promise is yet another mystery: "We shall not all sleep, but we shall all be changed." The insight revealed here refers to the gathering of believers to the Lord in the last days. Those who have died will experience resurrection, and those who are alive at this time in history will be transformed, so that all will be clothed with a new body like that of Christ, designed for life unending in heaven.

> For the Lord Himself will descend from heaven with a shout, with the voice of an archangel, and with the trumpet of God. And the dead in Christ will rise first. Then we who are alive and remain shall be caught up together with them in the clouds to meet the Lord in the air. And thus we shall always be with the Lord. Therefore comfort one another with these words. (1 Thessalonians 4:16–18)

With the last vestige of the curse removed from Adam's race, the rest of the earthly creation will be set free from the curse as well. Through the work of Christ, all the pain and suffering and death that have afflicted the animals since creation will be undone. By our obedience now, we can share in the redemption of the animal kingdom from the curse that our disobedience brought upon it. In this way, we can participate in the redemption of creation.

The Angels and the Believer

In the spiritual realm, we noted at the beginning of this chapter that God is using us to reveal His mysteries and His glory to the "principalities and powers in the heavenly places." This truth applies to both heavenly angels and fallen angels. Peter tells us that the heavenly angels desire to "look into" the remarkable truths of the gospel (1 Peter 1:12). It is fascinating to consider that these angels, who were the first to proclaim the arrival of the Messiah (Matthew 1:20–21; Luke 1:26–38, 2:9–14), seek to understand the mystery of the gospel.

Paul told the Corinthians that "we shall judge angels" (1 Corinthians 6:3). The angels described here are the fallen angels—the demons. This predicted experience will in part be the result of our being joined to Christ, who will be the Judge. Perhaps this judgment may also take the form of our being the means by which God exposes the satanic agenda. The attempts by Satan and his demons to harm, hinder, and kill those who are beloved of God and obey Him actually incur the wrath and judgment of our heavenly Father.

In the opening chapter of Job, Satan, while accusing Job, may actually be attempting to construct his own defense. Perhaps he is proposing that if all incentives to worship and submit to God were removed, any mortal would choose to be his own god. This choice would then prove that God is not intrinsically worthy of worship and authority, in which case Satan could justify his own rebellion.

Every time a believer in the midst of pain and helplessness receives grace to trust our heavenly Father, then choosing to submit to His will and being convinced of His love and His sovereignty, Satan and his minions stand condemned. Lucifer, who has stood in the presence of God, has seen His glory, His beauty, and His love, chose to rebel. These weak, witless, helpless, clueless mortals, who have never seen the face of God, choose to trust Him. Our choice may be one way in which we participate in the judgment of angels.

The mystery of God unfolding in our lives brings outcomes far greater than those we experience individually. It is possible that our response in the furnace of affliction may well be used by God to help convict and destroy the one who has caused all our pain, all our grief, all oppression and cruelty in the world.

Accepting the furnace in our lives may produce spiritual results that shake principalities and powers just as it did in Job's life. After all that he endured, Job proclaimed that God's purposes cannot be thwarted and they can be trusted. He chose to submit to God and to trust God. Once again, God is justified as the great I Am, and Satan's claims against God are defeated.

Expectations: What Does the Future Hold for Us?

> That I may know Him and the power of His resurrection, and the fellowship of His sufferings, being conformed to His death, if, by any means, I may attain to the resurrection from the dead. Not that I have already attained, or am already perfected; but I press on, that I may lay hold of that for which Christ Jesus has also laid hold of me. Brethren, I do not count myself to have apprehended; but one thing I do, forgetting those things which are behind and reaching forward to those things which are ahead, I press on toward the goal for the prize of the upward call of God in Christ Jesus. (Philippians 3:10–14)

Many people have come to us after searching for answers regarding disappointments in life. They feel discouraged by the past and apprehensive of the future. Things have not turned out the way they expected in their family, marriage, career, or relationship with God. One of the most profound questions one such seeker ever asked me was, "What am I to expect?"

As I searched the Scriptures for an answer, I discovered that perhaps this is the underlying question of the entire study of theology: what are we to expect of God, of ourselves, and of life? If this observation is true, then it might help explain some of the theological debates we often encounter. What if many of the most difficult theological conflicts come not from failing to find the right answer, but from failing to ask the right question? That is, instead of asking some form of the right question,

"What am I to expect of life?", we ask the wrong question: "How can I increase my knowledge so that I can increase my control?"

> Knowledge puffs up, but love builds up. (1 Corinthians 8:1b)

The Rapture

One persistent theological debate surrounds the question of the rapture (the taking up of believers to be with Christ) and the tribulation (the prophesied global disaster that will come upon the earth in the end times). The word *rapture* comes from the Latin translation of the Greek word in 1 Thessalonians 4:17 which the English renders as "caught up." It is also the term from which we derive the English word *raptor,* meaning a bird of prey. We are reminded of the marvelous scene from Tolkien's *Lord of the Rings* in which the hobbits, after completing their mission, are trapped on the volcano of Mount Doom as it begins to erupt. When all hope seems lost, the great eagles descend, snatch them up off the face of the mountain, and carry them to the king and to safety.

In attempting to understand the sequence of these prophesied events, scholars are divided over whether they believe the rapture will occur before (pretribulation), during (midtribulation), or after (posttribulation) the period of great tribulation. But what is our intent in examining the passages in question? If our intent is to gain knowledge for the purpose of control or intellectual pride, that is, to obtain the secret knowledge by which we feel superior, answers will elude us. On the other hand, if our intent is to find reassurance of God's protection and provision, then the answers will be given to us. The question changes from an academic one—"Exactly what will happen and when?"— to one of personal expectation: "Can we expect suffering?" and "Will God protect us?" The answer from the Scriptures is that every generation is to expect to share in the sufferings of Christ, and we can also expect His comfort, protection, and grace to endure and overcome the suffering. Furthermore, we can expect God to take whatever we experience (even that which is intended for evil by our enemies) and use it for good (Genesis 50:20). The answer God gives is "Fear not!" Prophecy is intended to give us neither anxiety nor control, but instead, secure anticipation. The intent of the passage which describes the rapture (1 Thessalonians 4:16–18) is clearly stated in verse 18: "Therefore comfort one another with these words."

Predestination

Another theological debate that has raged for centuries concerns the concepts of predestination and free will. Do believers choose to believe, or are they predestined by God to believe? If our intent is to master the deep knowledge of God and feel more control over our relationship with Him, the Scriptures will yield no answer. If our intent is finding security in our relationship with Him or finding hope for the salvation of a loved one, then the question has changed, and the answer is clear:

> Blessed be the God and Father of our Lord Jesus Christ, who has blessed us with every spiritual blessing in the heavenly places in Christ, just as he chose us in Him before the foundation of the world, that we should be holy and blameless before Him. In love He predestined us to adoption as sons through Jesus Christ to Himself, according to the kind intention of His will, to the praise of the glory of His grace, which He freely bestowed on us in the Beloved . . . also we have obtained an inheritance, having been predestined according to His purpose who works all things after the counsel of His will, to the end that we who were the first to hope in Christ should be to the praise of His glory . . . with a view to the redemption of God's own possession, to the praise of His glory. (Ephesians 1:3–6, 11–12, 14b, NASB)

In this first chapter of Ephesians, one of the most extensive teachings on predestination in the Bible, Paul repeats God's intention three times:

"to the praise of His glory." Also, predestination is put in the context of an "inheritance." This context suggests that those who are legitimate children are heirs to the inheritance.

> But God, being rich in mercy, because of His great love with which He loved us,
>
> Even when we were dead in our transgressions, made us alive together with Christ (by grace you have been saved), and raised us up with Him, and seated us with Him in the heavenly places, in Christ Jesus, in order that in the ages to come he might show the surpassing riches of His grace in kindness toward us in Christ Jesus. (Ephesians 2:4–7, NASB)

The Scriptures that pertain to predestination are intended for the security of the believer and the manifestation of the mercy, grace, and glory of God, not for speculation on the fate of individuals. In the first chapter of Ephesians, Paul describes our predestination to adoption, and it is in this context that he speaks of "the mystery of His will" (Ephesians 1:9). Here we revisit our study of God's will and are reminded that this matter is truly in God's circle—and we can trust Him with it.

The gates of heaven have often been described as having over the entrance, facing outward, a sign which reads: "Whosoever will, let him take of the water of life freely" (Revelation 22:17, KJV). Then, upon entering and looking back, there is a sign over the entrance facing inward which reads: "He chose us in Him before the foundation of the world" (Ephesians 1:4).

To enjoy the Scriptures as the living Word of God, let us study both the *con*tent and the *in*tent. Paul's conclusion to his teaching about foreknowledge and predestination in Romans 8 is this:

> For I am persuaded that neither death nor life, nor angels nor principalities nor powers, nor things present nor things to

> come, nor height nor depth, nor any other created thing, shall be able to separate us from the love of God which is in Christ Jesus our Lord. (Romans 8:38–39)

God is inviting us to find comfort not in our understanding or knowledge, but in Him alone. As a junior in college, when I was told my mother had Lou Gehrig's Disease and was dying, I remember praying, "God, if you will just tell me what you are going to do, whether you intend to heal her or take her home, I can trust you for that." It was as if He answered, "Ray, can you trust me for who I am rather than trusting the knowledge of My plan?"

> Therefore, let those also who suffer according to the will of God entrust their souls to a faithful Creator in doing what is right. (1 Peter 4:19, NASB)

The More Relevant Question

God's pattern in answering our questions is first to bring us to the place of asking the more relevant question. We looked earlier at John 9:1–3, where the disciples asked Jesus, "Who sinned, this man or his parents, that he was born blind?" Jesus' response revealed that they had asked the wrong question. They assumed they understood what the Bible had to say about sickness and neglected to discover the intention of God.

A similar story is told in John 8. A woman caught in the act of adultery was brought to Jesus. The Pharisees who brought her pointed out that her behavior was a violation of the law of Moses and that the penalty was stoning. Their question was, "What do you say?" (John 8:5). Their intent was to trap Jesus into either advocating that the law be ignored or accepting their interpretation and application of the law to this situation, thus endorsing their rule over the people. Jesus discerned both their evil intent and the need of the moment. He applied a more relevant principle of the law: that God alone is Judge (conviction of sin is in His circle). Their intent in using the law was not to glorify God, but to increase their control. Jesus in effect was teaching us to ask the question, "How does God want me to respond to this person now?" His response was not to ignore or minimize the law, but to do the opposite. He expanded the law beyond behavior to intent.

> He who is without sin among you, let him throw a stone at her first. (John 8:7)

Jesus is actually citing the very part of the law they were attempting to use (Deuteronomy 17:7, NIV). After stating that the witnesses are to be the first to begin the execution, this passage goes on to say, "You must purge the evil from among you." Jesus applies it as God intended it to be applied to reveal His holiness and our desperate bondage to sin. In this way, the law drives us to Him to be set free from this bondage. To fulfill the intent of the law, these accusers must deal with the evil among them, which includes the evil in themselves. This incident concludes with the Pharisees slinking away in shame and Jesus saying to the woman, "Neither do I condemn you; go and sin no more" (John 8:11). Jesus knows that He will soon pay for her sin. He is not dismissing sin, but instead taking it upon Himself. In essence, He is saying to the Pharisees, "Yes, her sin is worthy of death; and so is yours. If you stone her, you must also stone yourselves. If, however, you come to me, I will die in your place and you can be forgiven."

Jesus shows us that we are to respond to people, not react to an issue. The Pharisees kept trying to force Jesus to debate the issues. He consistently redirected them to discern the hearts. For this, we need the mind of Christ (1 Corinthians 2:16b).

In 1 Thessalonians 5:14 (NASB), we are told:

> And we urge you, brethren, admonish the unruly, encourage the fainthearted, help the weak, be patient with all men.

How to Respond

We need Christ's wisdom and discernment to know one from the other. We need Him to reveal to us who needs to be confronted (the unruly), who needs to be comforted (the fainthearted), and who needs to be carried (the weak). To "be patient with all men" implies we are also to wait upon God's timing to determine *when* to confront, comfort, or carry. Some who appear to be unruly may actually be discouraged or depressed. When others rebuke them, they are harming them and will incur God's judgment, like Job's friends. On the other hand, the unruly are often in pain because of their willfulness and pride. Those who are merciful but without discernment will respond to this pain by extending comfort when God intends confrontation. Well-intended mercy may actually serve to aid and abet the enemy in keeping a believer in bondage. This too may bring judgment, even upon an entire congregation (1 Corinthians 5:1–6). We cannot trust our understanding to know which Scripture to apply to which situation. Only God can show us how and when to respond to the person before us—what response will best meet the need and most glorify (reveal) God.

> If any of you lacks wisdom, let him ask of God, who gives to all liberally and without reproach, and it will be given to him. (James 1:5)

The Prayer of Jesus

On the eve of His crucifixion, Jesus prayed to His heavenly Father. This prayer is the most intimate revelation we have of the heart of Jesus. In this beautiful discourse, we are privileged to see the intentions of Jesus for all those who join with Him. In this prayer we are shown what to expect.

> Father, the hour has come. Glorify your Son, that Your Son also may glorify You, as You have given Him authority over all flesh, that He should give eternal life to as many as You have

> given Him. And this is eternal life, that they may know You, the only true God, and Jesus Christ whom You have sent.
>
> I pray for them. I do not pray for the world but for those whom You have given Me, for they are Yours . . . keep through Your Name those whom You have given Me, that they may be one as we are . . . that they may have my joy fulfilled in themselves.
>
> I do not pray that You should take them out of the world, but that You should keep them from the evil one. Sanctify them by Your Truth. Your Word is truth.
>
> I do not pray for these alone, but also for those who will believe in Me through their word; that they all may be one, as You, Father, are in Me, and I in You; that they also may be one in Us, that the world may believe that You sent Me.
>
> Father I desire that they also whom You gave Me may be with Me where I am, that they may behold My glory which You have given Me; for You loved Me before the foundation of the world. And I have declared to them Your name, and will declare it, that the love with which You loved Me may be in them, and I in them. (John 17:1–3, 9, 11b, 13b, 15, 17, 20–21, 24, 26)

Here, Jesus is praying for all those who will ever believe in Him. Through this prayer of intercession, He is giving us His protection, joy, love, sanctification (setting us apart and making us holy), eternal life—which is knowing Him intimately forever—and Himself, His very presence within us. He secures our future: "that they be with Me where I am." You may be fully assured that the prayer of Jesus Christ is being answered as you read these words.

> . . . the mystery which has been hidden from ages and from generations, but now has been revealed to His saints. To

> them God willed to make known what are the riches of the glory of this mystery among the Gentiles [the nations]: which is Christ in you, the hope of glory. (Colossians 1:26–27)

The Death Camp

There are many who stumble at the notion of God sending some to heaven and some to hell. But it is not a matter of God deciding at the end of our lives whether to send us to heaven or hell. Instead, the reality revealed by the Bible is that we are born into a prison camp—a death camp. If we remain in this camp, we will die spiritually. Growing up in a prison camp, we become acclimated to bondage. Having no other frame of reference, we think prison is normal; that it is reality. What do we come to expect in this place?

> That at that time you were without Christ, being aliens from the commonwealth of Israel and strangers from the covenants of promise, having no hope and without God in the world. (Ephesians 2:12)

The gospel is God through Christ opening the prison—bursting through its gates and making a way of escape. We must now respond to this opportunity. It is our choice to be made free or to remain in bondage.

Some will conclude that this opening of the gate and the one urging us to come to Him cannot be real, or it must be a trick of some kind. So they shrink farther back into the darkness and the false security of what is familiar. They demand proof of the reality of the claims of this "liberator." They proclaim that it is obvious to the intelligent that the notion of a "prison" is just an old myth. "Now that we are enlightened, we find this myth offensive and discriminatory. Those who continue to talk about it are guilty of hate speech and need to be silenced, punished, or reeducated. At least they should keep their beliefs to themselves."

Some will accept the truth of the prison but say that this liberation is unfair in determining when, where, and how the escape must take place. They demand to make their own gate where they prefer it to be, then debate among themselves to determine what conditions are required of those who wish to exit. Others will expect to earn release by good behavior. But of course, no one was ever released from a death camp for good behavior.

Some will believe that escape is not the solution. Instead, the prison should be reformed and turned into a resort of their own design. "If we all work together, we can turn this death camp into a heaven on earth."

Some are so distracted by their struggles in trying to meet their own needs and the needs of their loved ones that they ignore the gate altogether. "We don't have time to dream about what lies outside; we must survive in here. We must be realistic."

> The Spirit of the Lord God is upon Me,
> Because the Lord has anointed Me
> To preach good tidings to the poor;
> He has sent Me to heal the brokenhearted,
> To proclaim liberty to the captives,
> And the opening of the prison to those who are bound.
> (Isaiah 61:1)

This was the text used by Jesus in His first sermon in Nazareth. He began the sermon by saying, "Today this scripture is fulfilled in your hearing" (Luke 4:21).

> Jesus said to him, "I am the way, the truth, and the life. No one comes to the Father except through Me." (John 14:6)

> I am the door. If anyone enters by Me, he will be saved . . .
> I have come that they may have life, and that they may have it more abundantly. (John 10:9a, 10b)

The gospel, the good news, is not about conversion to a religion. This truth is poignantly revealed in the response of the dying criminal crucified beside Jesus. He was not told what system of beliefs he must accept, what theology he must understand, or what procedure by which to perform a conversion. Instead, he recognized Jesus as innocent, as loving him, and as a king who could somehow save him as he cried out,

> "Lord remember me when You come into Your kingdom." And Jesus said to him, "Assuredly, I say to you, today you will be with Me in Paradise." (Luke 23:41–42)

The gospel of Jesus Christ is an invitation more akin to a marriage proposal than to a religious conversion (2 Corinthians 11:2–3, Ephesians 5:31–32). It is an invitation to a relationship over against religion—all religion. It is not about a conversion from another religion to "Christianity"; it is about entering into a supernatural relationship with the living Christ, the source of all life and all love. A relationship He initiates, maintains, and completes. We then become a part of this glorious mystery that takes us through time into eternity with Him. We ultimately discover that all the treasures we seek are hidden in Christ Himself.

> . . . that their hearts may be encouraged, being knit together in love, and attaining to all the riches of the full assurance of understanding, to the knowledge of the mystery of God, both of the Father and of Christ, in whom are hidden all the treasures of wisdom and knowledge. (Colossians 2:2–3)

> My soul, wait silently for God alone,
> For my expectation is from Him.
> (Psalm 62:5)

And so we come back to the ultimate question: in this relationship with the living Christ, what am I to expect?

- I do not expect my flesh to improve with age (Psalm 73:26).
- I expect my flesh to do what it has always done and think as it has always thought (Romans 7:18, Galatians 5:17).
- I do not expect God to indulge my fleshly nature (Hebrews 12:6).
- I expect God to free me from being controlled by my fleshly nature (Romans 8:2, Galatians 5:16).
- I expect to increasingly find my identity in the spiritual nature (Romans 8:9–13, Galatians 5:16).
- I expect God to continue to expose my fears through situations of helplessness and to displace my fears with trust in Him (James 1:2-4, 1 Peter 4:12–13).
- I expect Him to teach me the fear of the Lord (Psalm 34:11).
- I do not expect to grow stronger, for I must decrease and He must increase (John 3:30).
- I do expect Him to perfect His strength in my weakness (2 Corinthians 12:9, Isaiah 40:29–31, 2 Corinthians 4:7–5:9).
- I do not expect less conflict or fewer trials (2 Timothy 2:3, 3:12).
- I do expect sufficient grace for every conflict and every trial (2 Corinthians 12:9, 2 Timothy 3:10–11).
- I expect God to remove the fear of suffering so that I am no longer intimidated by the threats of our enemy (Isaiah 41:10, Philippians 4:11–13).
- I do not expect a map of God's plan for my life (Psalm 37:23, Proverbs 16:9, Jeremiah 10:23).
- I do expect God to be my constant guide and provide a light for my path (Proverbs 3:5–6, Psalm 119:105).
- I expect God to remove obstructions in my mind and heart that interfere with knowing Him intimately (2 Corinthians 10:4–5).

- I do not expect my spouse or others to meet my needs (Psalm 62:5).
- I do expect God to fill my life and meet my needs (Ecclesiastes 5:20, Matthew 6:33).
- I do not expect myself to meet the needs of my spouse and others I love (John 15:5, Jeremiah 17:5–8).
- I expect Jesus to meet all the needs of those I love as I offer myself to be an available vessel of His provision (Philippians 4:13, Colossians 3:8–17).
- I expect to delight myself in the Lord (Psalm 37:4).
- I expect Him to give me the desires of my heart in His timing and on His terms, for they are always best (Psalm 37:4–11).
- I do not expect a "normal" life (Psalm 139:1–24, Isaiah 54:1–17, 1 Corinthians 2:9).
- I do expect a supernatural life that cannot be explained in human terms (Psalm 139:1–24, Isaiah 54:1–17, 1 Corinthians 2:9).
- I expect Him to protect my heart (Philippians 4:7).
- I expect His courage in my cowardice, His presence in my loneliness, His comfort in my grief, His forgiveness in my resentment, His faith in my doubt, His love in my indifference, His joy in my anxiety, His hope in my despair (Colossians 2:10, 1 Corinthians 2:3–5, 2 Corinthians 12:9, Psalm 73:26, Galatians 5:22–23).
- I do not expect appreciation from those to whom I minister (Matthew 6:2, Romans 2:29).
- I do expect and long to hear His voice one day saying, "Well done my good and faithful servant" (Matthew 25:23).
- I expect Him to glorify (reveal) Himself in me (Romans 8:29, 1 Corinthians 3:16, 1 Corinthians 1:26–31, 2 Corinthians 4:7).
- I expect to be continually surprised by God (1 Corinthians 2:9–12).
- I expect to see the goodness of the Lord in the land of the living (Psalm 27:13).
- I expect, when His purpose for me is fulfilled, to awaken in His presence and there to behold His face, feel His embrace, and enjoy

Him forever (Revelation 22:4–5, Psalm 73:23–24, 1 Corinthians 15:51–57, 1 Thessalonians 4:15–18).

In light of these expectations, we offer a prayer for the reader of this book:

May God give you grace (1 Corinthians 15:10):
To *see* the invisible (Hebrews 11:1, 2 Corinthians 4:18)
And *hear* the inaudible (John 10:3–5, Romans 8:26),
In order for you
To *know* the unknowable (Ephesians 3:18–19, Philippians 4:7,
1 Corinthians 2:9)
And *do* the impossible (Philippians 4:13, Matthew 17:20).

May you "Grow in grace and in the knowledge of our Lord and Saviour, Jesus Christ. To Him be glory both now and for ever. Amen" (2 Peter 3:18, KJV).

ENDNOTES

1. Lewis Sperry Chafer, *Systematic Theology.* Dallas, TX: Dallas Seminary Press, 1980. Volume IV, pp. 178–179; Volume V, pp. 315–347.

2. John Bowlby, *Attachment and Loss, Volume II: Separation.* 2nd Edition. New York: Basic Books: A division of HarperCollins Publishers, 1973. pp. 201–204.

3. C.S. Lewis, "The Business of Heaven," *The Inspirational Writings of C.S. Lewis.* New York, New York: Inspirational Press 1984. p. 475.

4. De Vaux, Roland. *Ancient Israel, Volume 2: Religious Institutions.* New York, New York: McGraw-Hill 1965. p.445.

5. Victor E. Frankl, *Man's Search for Meaning: An Introduction to Logotherapy.* Boston, MA: Beacon Press, 1974. p. 210.

6. Canter, Lee. *Assertive Discipline Parent Resource Guide.* Santa Monica, CA: Lee Canter and Assoc., 1985. pp.30-33.

7. Hendricks, Howard. Lecture notes, Dallas, TX: Dallas Theological Seminary. 1981.

8. Tolkien, J.R.R. *The Lord of the Rings.* New York, NY: Ballantine Books, 1965.

9. Lewis Sperry Chafer, *Systematic Theology.* Dallas, TX: Dallas Seminary Press. 1980. Volume II, p. 296.

10. Lewis Sperry Chafer, *Systematic Theology.* Dallas, TX: Dallas Seminary Press. 1980. Volume II, pp. 283–315.

11. Noah Webster, *Webster's Third New International Dictionary: Volume 1,* Springfield, MA: G. & C. Merriam Co. 1971. p.760.

12. Dr. Charles Stanley. Sermon notes from personal collection.

13. Anthony Kenney, *Wyclif.* Oxford, UK: Oxford University Press, 1985. p. 63.

14. Tim Dowley, ed. *Eerdmans' Handbook to the History of Christianity.* Grand Rapids, Michigan: Wm B. Eerdmans Publishing Co., 1977. p. 364.

INDEX OF SCRIPTURES

1

2

A

H

I

J

L

M

N

P

R

Z

BIBLIOGRAPHY

Addison, J. Ray. *Perceptions of Control and Responsibility as Factors in the Revictimization of Adult Survivors of Childhood Sexual Abuse.* PhD. diss., Oxford Graduate School. 1992.

Addison, Susan C. *The Effects of Gender, Attachment Style, and Locus of Control on the Experience and Expression of Anger.* PhD. diss., Oxford Graduate School. 1994.

Addison, Susan C. *The Development of Identity and Ministry for Christian Women in the Local Church A.D. 1980–2000.* Master's thesis, Dallas Theological Seminary. 1983.

Aland, Kurt, et. al., eds. *The Greek New Testament.* 3rd Edition. New York: American Bible Society, 1975.

Bauer, Walter. *A Greek-English Lexicon of the New Testament. 2nd Edition* Revised and augmented by William F. Arndt and F. Wilbur Gingrich. Chicago: The University of Chicago Press, 1979.

Berry, George R. *Berry's Interlinear Greek-English New Testament.* Grand Rapids, MI: Guardian Press, 1976.

Bowlby, John. *Attachment and Loss, Volume II: Separation.* 2nd Edition. New York: Basic Books, a division of HarperCollins Publishers, 1973.

Brown, Francis, S.R. Driver, and Charles A. Briggs. *A Hebrew and English Lexicon of the Old Testament.* Oxford, UK: Clarendon Press, 1979.

Canter, Lee. *Assertive Discipline for Parents.* Santa Monica, CA: Lee Canter and Assoc., 1985.

Canter, Lee. *Assertive Discipline Parent Resource Guide.* Santa Monica, CA: Lee Canter and Assoc., 1985.

Chafer, Lewis Sperry. *Systematic Theology.* Dallas, TX: Dallas Seminary Press. 1980.

De Vaux, Roland. *Ancient Israel, Volume 2: Religious Institutions.* New York, New York: McGraw-Hill, 1965.

Dowley, Tim. ed. *Eerdmans' Handbook to the History of Christianity.* Grand Rapids, Michigan:Wm B. Eerdmans Publishing Co., 1977.

Frankl, Victor E. *Man's Search for Meaning: An Introduction to Logotherapy.* Boston, MA: Beacon Press, 1974.

Gesenius' *Hebrew and Chaldee Lexicon to the Old Testament Scriptures.* Translated by Samuel P. Tregelles. Grand Rapids, Michigan: Wm. B. Eerdmans Publishing Co, 1976.

Green, J.P. Sr., ed. *The New Englishman's Greek Concordance and Lexicon.* Peabody, MA: Hendrickson Publishers, 1982.

Hendricks, Howard. Lecture notes, Dallas, TX: Dallas Theological Seminary. 1981.

Kenney, Anthony. *Wyclif.* Oxford University Press: Oxford, UK 1985.

Lewis, C.S. "The Business of Heaven," *The Inspirational Writings of C.S. Lewis.* New York, New York: Inspirational Press, 1984.

Newton, John. "Amazing Grace," *The Hymnal for Worship & Celebration.* Waco, TX: Word Music, 1986.

Rosen, Ceil and Moshe Rosen. *Christ in the Passover.* Chicago, IL: Moody Press, 1978.

Strong, James. *Strong's Exhaustive Concordance.* Nashville, TN: Crusade Bible Publishers, 1976.

Thayer, Joseph Henry. *Greek-English Lexicon of the New Testament.* Grand Rapids, Michigan: Zondervan, 1976.

Tolkien, J.R.R. *The Lord of the Rings.* New York, NY: Ballantine Books, 1965.

Webster, Noah. *Webster's Third New International Dictionary.* Volume 1. Springfield, MA: G. & C. Merriam Co., 1971.

The year she turned sixty, Susan Addison was blazing around Daytona Speedway behind the wheel of a Mazda RX-8 in the season opener of the Grand-Am Rolex Sports Car Series. Ray was in the pit, praying.

Ray was drawn to Susan by her faith and her laughter; Susan was drawn to Ray's wisdom and heart for discipleship. The couple met in New Orleans at Berean Bible Church, where Susan discipled nursing students and Ray ministered to youth while finishing his MDiv at the Baptist Seminary. Susan graduated with honors from Dallas Theological Seminary, where they both studied under Dr. Frank Minirth and Dr. Paul Meier. After working with Minirth-Meier Clinic, Ray earned an MS in Counseling from Texas A&M. Susan and Ray both completed their PhDs in Religion and Society/Behavioral Science at Oxford Graduate School.

Today, the Addisons enjoy living in the foothills of the Blue Ridge Mountains and continue in private practice. Susan still longs to be racing; Ray is still praying.